Lecture Notes in Computer Science 13754

More information about this series at https://link.springer.com/bookseries/558

Luigi Manfredi · Seyed-Ahmad Ahmadi ·
Michael Bronstein · Anees Kazi ·
Davide Lomanto · Alwyn Mathew ·
Ludovic Magerand · Kamilia Mullakaeva ·
Bartlomiej Papiez · Russell H. Taylor ·
Emanuele Trucco (Eds.)

Imaging Systems for GI Endoscopy, and Graphs in Biomedical Image Analysis

First MICCAI Workshop, ISGIE 2022
and Fourth MICCAI Workshop, GRAIL 2022
Held in Conjunction with MICCAI 2022
Singapore, September 18, 2022
Proceedings

Editors
Luigi Manfredi 🆔
University of Dundee
Dundee, UK

Seyed-Ahmad Ahmadi 🆔
Nvidia
Munich, Germany

Michael Bronstein
University of Oxford
Oxford, UK

Anees Kazi
Harvard University
Boston, USA

Davide Lomanto 🆔
National University of Singapore
Singapore, Singapore

Alwyn Mathew
University of Dundee
Dundee, UK

Ludovic Magerand
University of Dundee
Dundee, UK

Kamilia Mullakaeva
Technical University of Munich
Munich, Germany

Bartlomiej Papiez 🆔
University of Oxford
Oxford, UK

Russell H. Taylor
Johns Hopkins University
Baltimore, USA

Emanuele Trucco
University of Dundee
Dundee, UK

ISSN 0302-9743   ISSN 1611-3349 (electronic)
Lecture Notes in Computer Science
ISBN 978-3-031-21082-2   ISBN 978-3-031-21083-9 (eBook)
https://doi.org/10.1007/978-3-031-21083-9

This Springer imprint is published by the registered company Springer Nature Switzerland AG
The registered company address is: Gewerbestrasse 11, 6330 Cham, Switzerland

ISGIE Preface

The First International on Imaging Systems for GI Endoscopy (ISGIE 2022) was organized as a satellite event of the 25th International Conference on Medical Image Computing and Computer Assisted Intervention (MICCAI 2022) in Singapore, and held on September 18, 2022, as a half-day event.

This workshop was specific to the application of imaging systems in the gastrointestinal (GI) tract. The objective of this event was to stimulate an interdisciplinary discussion on clinical applications focusing on unmet clinical needs as well as on new technologies at the R&D stage, aiming for translation into clinical practice. Both clinical and engineering communities benefit from these discussions, which fit with the MICCAI mission.

This workshop focused on novel scientific contributions on vision systems, imaging algorithms, and autonomous systems for endorobots for GI endoscopy, including lesion and lumen detection as well as 3D reconstruction of the GI tract. Localizing interesting features such as the lumen, lesions, or polyps to be removed, requires their detection in the images of the video stream. Deep learning-based approaches of this task have become very successful in recent years, with annotated datasets publicly available to train them. Challenges remain, especially concerning the robustness of the illumination because of the reflective surface. Potential solutions to these issues were discussed in this workshop. Another important aspect in endoscopy, covered in this workshop, was the level of autonomy of a medical device to support the clinical workforce in performing the procedure. This autonomous behavior can benefit from 3D information such as the localization of the target, lumen, or lesion, and the position of a device with respect to the wall of the GI tract. Traditionally this information could be obtained from a monocular video system by using methods such as SLAM, shape-from-template, and non-rigid structure-from-motion. More recently, methods based on deep learning monocular depth estimation also have emerged. This workshop addressed progress made with those approaches and limitations remaining to successfully move a device autonomously as well as achieving autonomous surgical tasks.

The workshop consisted of the presentation of six selected papers and three invited keynote talks covering both clinical and technical aspects. A technical talk was given by Russell Taylor, Professor of Computer Science with joint appointments in Mechanical Engineering, Otolaryngology Head-and-Neck Surgery, Radiology, and Surgery and Director of the Laboratory for Computational Sensing and Robotics (LCSR) at Johns Hopkins University. He provided an overview of current research and technologies together with new trends and future technologies, including autonomy in medicine.

Another technical talk was also given by José María Martínez Montiel, Full Professor in the Department of Computer Science Systems Engineering at the University of Zaragoza, where he is in charge of perception and computer vision research grants and courses. He presented EndoMapper, a dataset of complete calibrated endoscopy procedures, which results from a funded European Union project, grant agreement No. 863146. He covered the important aspects of visual SLAM and the dataset provided by this project to simulate the colon environment and to provide synthetic data for training purposes. The clinical talk was given by Lawrence Ho Khek-Yu, Full Professor in the Department of Surgery at the National University of Singapore and the Director of the Centre for Innovation in Healthcare, National University Health System. He presented current solutions available in clinical practice, providing an in-depth view of unmet clinical needs. His talk covered the patient perspective and the acceptance of new technologies, such as AI and robotics, as well as challenges on equality and diversity in endoscopy.

The ISGIE 2022 proceedings contain six high-quality papers, selected from 9 submissions through a rigorous double-blind peer-review process, with three reviewers for each paper, all of them experts on the topic. Full authorship and domain conflicts were disclosed in CMT, the manuscript submission system, in order to avoid conflict of interest between authors and reviewers of the papers. The accepted manuscripts cover light adaptation for classification of the upper GI sites, criss-cross attention for GI metaplasia segmentation, landmark detection using vision transformers in colonoscopy, real-time lumen detection for autonomous colonoscopy, SuperPoint features in colonoscopy, and estimating coverage in 3D reconstruction of the colon from colonoscopy videos. We would like to thank all the ISGIE 2022 authors for their submissions and participation, the members of the organizing team, the reviewers, and the keynote speakers for their valuable contributions and commitment to the workshop. We would like to thank our sponsor Olympus for its support by funding an award of 1,000 USD for the best presentation, which went to O. León Barbed from DIIS-i3A, University of Zaragoza, Spain, for his talk on "SuperPoint Features in Endoscopy".

The proceedings of our workshop are published as a joint LNCS volume alongside the Fourth International Workshop on Graphs in Biomedical Image Analysis (GRAIL 2022), organized in conjunction with MICCAI. In addition to the papers, abstracts and slides presented during the workshop will be made publicly available on the ISGIE website (https://miccai2022-isgie.github.io/).

September 2022

Luigi Manfredi
Russell Taylor
Davide Lomanto
Alwyn Mathew
Ludovic Magerand
Emanuele Trucco

Preface GRAIL 2022

The Fourth International Workshop on GRaphs in biomedicAl Image anaLysis (GRAIL 2022) was organized as a satellite event of the 25th International Conference on Medical Image Computing and Computer Assisted Intervention (MICCAI 2022) in Singapore. Following two years of entirely virtual conference events, we were excited to offer our community a hybrid event, and finally meet some of our colleagues face-to-face again. After the success and positive feedback obtained in previous years, GRAIL had its fourth event at MICCAI 2022, in the spirit of strengthening the links between graphs and biomedical imaging.

This workshop provides a unique opportunity to meet and discuss both theoretical advances in graphical methods and the practicality of such methods when applied to complex biomedical imaging problems. Simultaneously, the workshop seeks to be an interface to foster future interdisciplinary research, including signal processing and machine learning on graphs.

Graphs and related graph-based modeling have attracted an exponentially growing research interest in recent years, as they enable us to represent complex data and their interactions in a perceptually meaningful way. With the emergence of big data in the medical imaging community, the relevance of graphs as a means to represent data sampled from irregular and non-Euclidean domains is increasing, together with the development of new inference and learning methods that operate on such structures. There is a wide range of well-established and emerging biomedical imaging problems that can benefit from these advances. We believe that the research presented at this workshop constitutes a clear example of that. Compared to our previous GRAIL events, we specifically encouraged submissions in the areas of explainable GNNs, graph models in computer-aided surgery/intervention, unstructured medical big data, and semantic knowledge (scene/knowledge graphs).

The GRAIL 2022 proceedings contain six high-quality papers of 9–10 pages that were pre-selected from 10 submissions in a rigorous peer-review process. All submissions were peer-reviewed in a double-blind process by at least three members of the reviewing board and Program Committee, comprising 20 experts on graphs in biomedical image analysis, with each member undertaking at least one review. The accepted manuscripts cover a wide set of graph-based medical image analysis methods and applications. As in previous years, one of the primary domains of imaging-related graph methods are brain connectomics. Papers this year proposed brain connectome encoding methods for anomaly detection and disease diagnosis; generation of post-surgical connectomes in tumor patients; multimodal brain connectome fusion methods; and transforming connectomes to arbitrary brain parcellations via graph matching. Outside of brain imaging, we saw an application of graphs for labeling of vasculature trees, and improved annotation of whole slide images in digital pathology with hierarchical cell-graphs.

In addition to the papers presented in this LNCS volume, the workshop event featured four outstanding keynote presentations from world-renowned experts: Marinka

Zitnik from Harvard Medical School on "Trustworthy AI with GNN Explainers", Mark O'Donoghue from Astra Zeneca on "Knowledge Graphs for Drug Discovery", Islem Rekik from the Technical University of Istanbul on "Debunking the brain connectivity using predictive learning from limited data", and Xavier Bresson from Sea AI Lab (formerly from the National University of Singapore) on "GNN trends in 2022".

We wish to thank all the GRAIL 2022 authors for their submissions and participation, the members of the Program Committee, the numerous reviewers, and of course the keynote speakers for their valuable contributions and commitment to the workshop. Finally, we are very grateful to our sponsor NVIDIA for their generous support, by awarding a GPU to the best workshop presentation.

The proceedings of our workshop are published as a joint LNCS volume alongside the First International Workshop on Imaging Systems for GI Endoscopy (ISGIE 2022), organized in conjunction with MICCAI. In addition to the papers, abstracts and slides presented during the workshop will be made publicly available on the GRAIL website (http://grail-miccai.github.io/).

September 2022

Seyed-Ahmad Ahmadi
Anees Kazi
Bartlomiej Papiez
Kamilia Mullakaeva
Michael Bronstein

Organization

General Chairs ISGIE 2022

Luigi Manfredi   University of Dundee, UK
Davide Lomanto   National University of Singapore
Russell Taylor   Johns Hopkins University, USA

Program Committee ISGIE 2022

Alwyn Mathew (Chair)   University of Dundee, UK
Ludovic Magerand (Chair) University of Dundee, UK
Emanuele Trucco (Chair)   University of Dundee, UK
Baidaa Al-Bander   Keele University, UK
Adrien Bartoli   Clermont University Hospital, France
Zhen Li   Chinese University of Hong Kong, Shenzhen and
                          Shenzhen Research Institute of Big Data
                          (SRIBD), China
Liu Li   Chinese University of Hong Kong, Shenzhen,
                          China
Arianna Menciassi   Scuola Superiore Sant'Anna of Pisa, Italy
Mathieu Pioch   CHU de Lyon, France

Additional Reviewers ISGIE 2022

Zixun Zhang   Jun Wei
Zhuo Li   Jie Yang
Yuncheng Jiang   Jacob Carse
Yiwen Hu   José María Martínez Montiel
Ye Zhu   Daniel Pizarro
Weizhen Ding   Behzad Mirmahboub
Weijie Ma   Agniva Sengupta
Marian Himstedt

Sponsors ISGIE 2022

We are very grateful to our sponsor Olympus for their valuable support and awarding
1,000 USD to the best paper.

General Chair GRAIL 2022

Seyed-Ahmad Ahmadi   NVIDIA GmbH, Germany

Program Committee Chairs GRAIL 2022

Seyed-Ahmad Ahmadi   NVIDIA GmbH, Germany
Anees Kazi   Harvard Medical School, USA
Bartłomiej W. Papież   University of Oxford, UK
Kamilia Mullakaeva   Technical University of Munich, Germany
Michael Bronstein   University of Oxford, UK

Additional Reviewers GRAIL 2022

Erik Bekkers   Matthias Keicher
Alaa Bessadok   Andrew Melbourne
Tobias Czempiel   Tamara Mueller
Vijay Prakash Dwivedi   Ege Özsoy
Azade Farshad   Roger Soberanis-Mukul
Mahsa Ghorbani   Gerome Vivar
Xiaoxin He   Yalin Wang
Felix Holm

Sponsor GRAIL 2022

We are very grateful to our sponsor NVIDIA for their valuable support and awarding a GPU to the best workshop presentation.

Contents

Imaging Systems for GI Endoscopy

Light Adaptation for Classification
of the Upper Gastrointestinal Sites

Xiaohan Hao, Xiao Xu, Daimin Jiang, and Guoyi Zhou[✉]

SonoScape Medical Corp., Shanghai, China
hxh045@mail.ustc.edu.cn, zhougy@sonoscape.net

Abstract. Plenty of computer-aided blind-spot monitoring systems based on the classification model of the upper gastrointestinal sites are developed to enhance the quality of gastroscopy. However, the performance of the white light (WL) based model drops deeply while changing the light source to the special light (SL), a narrowed-spectrum technology. A naive solution is to collect as much data from SL as from WL, but it is hard and time-consuming. In this work, we propose a novel light adaptive module that is only trained by common labeled WL images and unlabeled SL images. Our proposed structure is a plug-in module including a light classification head and a reconstruction decoder. The light classification head is trained in an adversarial manner, which prevents the backbone network to extract light-related features. The reconstruction decoder facilitates the complete preservation of the extracted structural features. The result showed that the original classification model added with our proposed light adaptive module could significantly improve the classification performance under SL and keep the original accuracy under WL, which may help endoscopists achieve better gastroscopy.

Keywords: Domain adaptation · Endoscopic image · Disentanglement

1 Introduction

Gastroscopy is a crucial examination for the detection and diagnosis of gastrointestinal lesions [1], but the quality of the gastroscopy is dependent on the level of endoscopists [2]. To improve the quality of gastroscopy, some computer-aided systems have been developed for monitoring blind spots during gastroscopy to ensure endoscopists do not neglect gastric cancers and precursor lesions [3,4]. One of the critical components of the system is a model for the classification of sites of the upper gastrointestinal tract, which achieves satisfactory accuracy under white light (WL). However, each endoscope manufacturer introduces its own unique special light (SL) source based on narrowed-spectrum technology to enhance images, such as narrow band imaging, blue laser imaging, i-Scan digital contrast, etc. [5]. When the endoscopists switch the light source during endoscopy, the proportion of light waves with different penetration depths is changed, which unveils different texture patterns on mucosal surfaces and vascular structures. Hence the performance of the blind-spot monitoring system which is trained on WL may drop heavily due to the domain shift.

L. Manfredi et al. (Eds.): ISGIE 2022/GRAIL 2022, LNCS 13754, pp. 3–12, 2022.
https://doi.org/10.1007/978-3-031-21083-9_1

To address the problem, a naive way is to collect as much data from SL as from WL. However, it is rare and time-consuming since endoscopists do not usually switch to SL mode except they need to clearly observe the tissues during a gastroscopic examination. The development of domain adaptation methods provides a new opportunity to improve the performance of monitoring blind spots under SL without enough labeled training data of SL. Mahmood et al. [6] proposed a framework that generates the synthetic images from real images to train the network which addresses the lack of annotated data. The framework was called reverse domain adaptation and successfully applied in-depth estimation for monocular endoscopy. Zeng et al. [17] proposed an unsupervised domain adaptation method based on intra- and cross-modality semantic consistency on hip joint bone segmentation and cardiac substructure segmentation. Perone et al. [18] extended the unsupervised domain adaptation method in a self-ensembling way to enhance the generalization of a model to other domains and verified the method in the gray matter segmentation task of magnetic resonance imaging. Those excellent researches demonstrated that domain adaptation technology could be successfully applied in various scenarios to address the lack of labeled data or improve the generalization of the model. To the best of our knowledge, it is the first time to apply domain adaptation methods for the classification of upper gastrointestinal sites under SL.

In this work, we proposed a light adaptive module (LAM) that could be plugged and played into a current existing convolutional neural network (CNN) to improve the generalization of the WL-based model under the SL. Concretely speaking, we added a light classification head and a reconstruction decoder to the original classification model. The light classification head is adversarial to the backbone network, which prevents the backbone network to extract the light-related feature by a gradient reversal layer. The decoder generates the illumination normalized grayscale image to help the backbone network preserve the structural feature which was useful for the classification of the upper gastrointestinal sites. During the inference phase, these additional modules do not need to work, that is, they do not increase any costs of the original model. The method works in a domain-agnostic manner, so no additional domain information is required during inference. In the video stream with a mix of WL and SL, the performance of the classification model trained by adding LAM hardly decreased under WL, but the performance under SL was greatly improved.

2   Methods

LAM is shown in Fig. 1, which is made up of a light classification head and a reconstruction decoder. LAM is a plug-and-play module that only adds to the existing classification model in the training phase and does not work in the inference phase, so LAM does not increase any costs to the original classification model. In this section, we make a detailed description of the proposed LAM.

2.1   Motivation

We define the light adaptation task as in the unsupervised homogeneous domain adaptation setting [8], that is, there is sufficient labeled data of the source domain (WL) but no labeled data of the target domain (SL) in the training dataset. We assume that the feature spaces and dimensions between WL and SL are identical, but the data distributions are different. In the homogeneous domain adaptation setting, discrepancy-based methods [9,10], adversarial-based methods [11,12], and reconstruction-based methods [13,14] are applied in general.

However, our task is a bit more complex than the abovementioned research since the SL data is not only expensive to annotate but also hard to collect. In this case, some methods like the generative model-based methods may not work well. Moreover, the abovementioned methods also assume that the model applies only in one domain, but in real clinic scenarios, the illumination can be changed at any moment, so the classification model must work in a mixed domain. Therefore, we designed LAM in a domain-agnostic manner [15]. We leverage the gradient reversal layer to remove the light-specific features extracted by the backbone network in an adversarial manner. The reconstruction decoder is employed to remain as complete light-invariant features as possible. The conventional classification head for upper gastrointestinal sites is trained by WL data to extract the class-relevant features based on the light-invariant features. Hence, no matter WL or SL, the input images can be transformed into the same feature space so as to avoid a domain shift.

2.2   Common Classification Model

Since a big success of Alex on Imagenet in 2012 [19], more and more excellent convolutional neural networks for classification have been developed, such as resnet [20], mobilenet [21], etc. Those networks are composed of a backbone network and a classification head. The backbone network is characterized by stacking many consecutive identical modules which are leveraged for feature extraction. After inputting an image to the backbone network, a feature map that is generally 32 times smaller than the original input is obtained. Subsequently, the feature map is fed to a classification head which contains a global average layer and a fully connected layer, and then the classification prediction result is got.

2.3   Light Classification Head

As shown in Fig. 1, the light classification head consists of a gradient reversal layer [7], a convolutional layer, a batch normalization layer, a rectified linear unit (ReLU) layer, and a convolutional layer. The last convolutional layer outputs an $N \times N \times L$ prediction map where $N \times N$ is the size of the final feature map of backbone network, and L is the number of light sources. We defined a light adaptive loss based on the output of the light classification head, which is a pixel-wise cross-entropy loss and written as

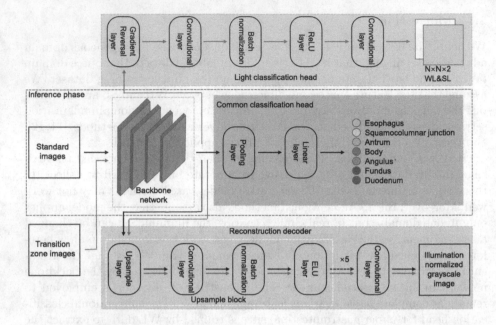

Fig. 1. The architecture of LAM. LAM could be plugged into conventional CNNs. LAM consists of a light classification head and a reconstruction decoder, which are trained by both annotated standard images and unlabelled transition zone images. During the inference phase, LAM is removed so no costs are increased.

$$L_{lc} = - \sum_{i,x,y} \left[L_i \times \log p_i^{(x,y)} + (1 - L_i) \times \log(1 - p_i^{(x,y)}) \right] \qquad (1)$$

where $p_i^{(x,y)}$ denotes the value of prediction map p generated by the light classification head of ith light source at location (x, y).

The gradient reversal layer is leveraged to make the backbone network adversarial to the light classification head. In the forward phase, the layer just represents an identity operator, while in the backpropagation phase, the sign of gradient is reversed. Hence, the network is trained in an adversarial manner, that is the light classification head minimizes the cross-entropy loss but the backbone network maximizes the loss at the same time.

2.4   Reconstruction Decoder

The reconstruction decoder is illustrated in Fig. 1. We define sequential layers as an upsample block including a upsample layer, a convolutional layer, a batch normalization layer, and an exponential linear unit (ELU) layer. Five upsample blocks and a convolutional layer stack together so that the final feature map of the backbone network can be zoomed to the original input size and the dimension is also transformed as the same as the input image. The weighted sum of MSE loss and SSIM loss [23] is considered the loss function of reconstruction, where the weight ratio of MSE loss to SSIM loss is 10:1.

It is obvious that there is a conflict between the light classification head and the reconstruction decoder because the function of the light classification head is to remove light-specific features whereas the function of the reconstruction decoder head is to preserve the whole information. Thus, through min-max normalization and grayscale transformation, we render the illumination normalized grayscale image of the original input as the reconstruction decoder ground-truth. Between WL images and SL images, the color, brightness, and texture pattern are changed due to the change of spectrum, which is apparent in Fig. 2. We assume that color-related and brightness-related features are not beneficial for the classification of upper gastrointestinal sites, so reconstruction to the illumination normalized grayscale image can alleviate the conflict between light classification head and reconstruction decoder as much as possible in terms of color-related and brightness-related features.

2.5 Implementation Details

During the training stage, each batch of the input images contains two parts. One is the standard photograph from a gastroscopic examination with the annotation of upper gastrointestinal sites. The other is the non-standard screenshots from the gastroscopic examination videos which do not belong to any set categories and thereby only have domain labels. The standard photographs with 24 batch size are used for calculating the cross-entropy loss for the classification of upper gastrointestinal sites. The non-standard screenshots with 16 batch size are utilized to calculate the light adaptive loss. All of the inputs are used to calculate reconstruction loss. Total loss is the sum of upper gastrointestinal sites classification loss, light adaptive loss, and reconstruction loss.

Since the light adaptive loss is a pixel-wise loss, it is necessary to cut out the black borders around the gastroscopic images to ensure every input pixel has the light source information. After cropping, the images are resized to 224×224 and augmented by a combination of procedures including the random horizontal flip, random change of brightness, hue, saturation, and value, and random cutout. The weight of the gradient reversal layer is 0.01. Adaptive moment estimation (Adam) algorithm [25] is selected as the optimizer with an initial learning rate of 0.0001. After consecutively training for 100 epochs, the checkpoint with maximum average accuracy in the validation cohort is considered the final model. Models are trained on a single RTX 2080 GPU via PyTorch [16] framework.

3   Experiments

3.1   Dataset

To construct the datasets, we collected a total of 1202 patients data with gastroscopic examination videos and frozen images using the HD-550 Video Endoscopy

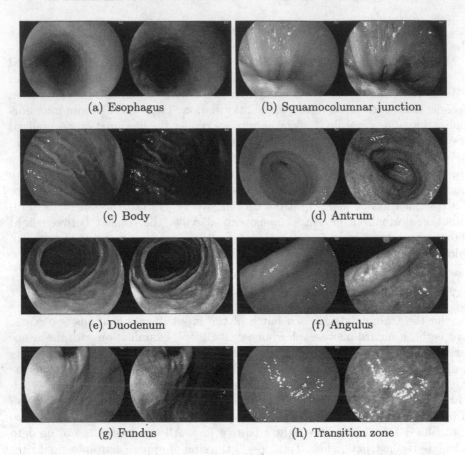

(a) Esophagus   (b) Squamocolumnar junction

(c) Body   (d) Antrum

(e) Duodenum   (f) Angulus

(g) Fundus   (h) Transition zone

Fig. 2. The illustration of different upper gastrointestinal sites. (a–g) are from frozen images. (h) is from screenshots of the gastroscopic video

System by Sonoscape. All of the patients were examined by both WL and Versatile Intelligent Staining Technology [24] which is defined as SL in this work. Enrolled patients were randomly split into training, validation, and test cohort in a ratio of 6:1:3, that is 720 patients in the training cohort, 121 patients in the validation cohort, and 361 patients in the test cohort. Frozen images were acquired by freezing operation when the endoscopist observe a clear and standard upper gastrointestinal site under WL or SL. An endoscopist with 5-year endoscopy experience annotated frozen images to 7 upper gastrointestinal sites. To train the LAM, we also captured 865 screenshots from examination videos in the training cohort which belongs to transition zones between the upper gastrointestinal sites. Some samples of the datasets are illustrated in Fig. 2. The frozen images were used for building the baseline model or models with LAM, as well as the evaluation of models. The transition zone images were only used to build the models with LAM. The specific image numbers of every upper gastrointestinal site are shown in Table 1.

Table 1. The numbers of upper gastrointestinal images in training and test cohort.

Dataset		Esophagus	SJ.	Antrum	Body	Angulus	Fundus	duodenum	Total
Training	WL images (for classification)	357	535	1204	2755	497	1550	1075	7973
	SL images (for LAM)	–	–	–	–	–	–	–	170
	WL images (for LAM)	–	–	–	–	–	–	–	695
Val	WL images	55	84	219	536	76	275	173	1418
Test	WL images	257	184	803	1964	363	1189	714	5474
	SL images	168	129	16	21	12	16	8	370

SJ is the abbreviation of squamocolumnar junction.

3.2 Experiment Details

We used ResNet-18 and ResNet-50 as backbone networks to evaluate the validity of the proposed LAM under WL and SL. Moreover, we performed an ablation study based on ResNet-50 to explore the respective roles of different heads. All of the models were trained in the same setting which was described in 2.5.

Table 2. The Accuracy of models under different light source.

Model		Esophagus	SJ.	Antrum	Body	Angulus	Fundus	duodenum	Mean
WL	ResNet-18	0.969	0.989	0.993	0.976	0.988	0.979	0.994	0.984
	ResNet-18+LAM	0.964	0.989	0.992	0.982	0.980	0.950	0.975	0.976
SL	ResNet-18	0.071	0.078	0.187	0.952	0.833	0.625	0.750	0.500
	ResNet-18+LAM	**0.643**	**0.473**	**0.625**	**1.000**	**0.917**	**0.687**	0.750	**0.728**
WL	ResNet-50	0.974	0.993	0.993	0.981	0.977	0.967	0.992	0.982
	ResNet-50+LAM	0.969	0.978	0.992	0.972	0.992	0.969	0.996	0.981
SL	ResNet-50	0.071	0.000	0.125	0.952	0.333	0.625	0.500	0.372
	ResNet-50+LAM	**0.768**	**0.543**	**0.687**	0.857	**0.833**	**0.687**	**1.000**	**0.768**

SJ is the abbreviation of squamocolumnar junction.

3.3 Results

The results are reported in Table 2. It is suggested that ResNet attached with LAM can improve the predictive performance significantly without external labeled data under SL. For the esophagus, squamocolumnar junction, antrum, and angulus, the prediction accuracy of the subclass under SL are also higher than that of the baseline model. In addition, the overall accuracy and the accuracy of a subclass under WL of the model with LAM are only slightly lower than the baseline model, which means adding LAM does not affect the original performance of the model. The results of the ablation study are given in Table 3. It indicates that introducing the light classification head and the reconstruction decoder can improve the classification performance of the model under SL, respectively.

The results show that our proposed model has the ability to recognize various upper gastrointestinal sites under both WL and SL, so it is capable of real clinic scenarios where upper gastrointestinal images under WL or SL are mixed in one video stream. Here we do not compare to other domain adaptation methods such as cyclegan [12] or adaBN [22], because those methods need to obtain additional domain information during the inference phase.

Table 3. Ablation study for LAM under SL.

Model	Esophagus	SJ	Antrum	Body	Angulus	Fundus	duodenum	Mean
ResNet-50	0.071	0.000	0.125	0.952	0.333	0.625	0.500	0.372
ResNet-50 + light classification head	0.167	0.310	0.312	1.000	0.833	0.625	1.000	0.607
ResNet-50 + light classification head + reconstruction decoder	0.768	0.543	0.687	0.857	0.833	0.687	1.000	0.768

SJ is the abbreviation of squamocolumnar junction.

4   Conclusion

In this study, we proposed a plug-and-play LAM module that aims to enhance the discriminating power for the classification of upper gastrointestinal sites under SL. LAM can be trained without any labeled SL data and does not work during the inference phase so that no cost is added. Our experimental results indicated that by adding the LAM, the performance under WL is only slightly decreased, but the accuracy under SL becomes significantly higher, which proves that LAM can decouple the light-specific features and light-invariant features, and facilitate the backbone network to extract class-related features. For future work, we intend to expand the number of datasets and types of light sources to more fully validate our proposed LAM and to develop more advanced modules for finer decoupling of image representations.

References

1. Bisschops, R., et al.: Performance measures for upper gastrointestinal endoscopy: a European Society of Gastrointestinal Endoscopy (ESGE) Quality Improvement Initiative. Endoscopy **48**, 843–864 (2016)
2. Rutter, M.D., Rees, C.J.: Quality in gastrointestinal endoscopy. Endoscopy **46**, 526–528 (2014)

3. Wu, L., et al.: Randomised controlled trial of WISENSE, a real-time quality improving system for monitoring blind spots during esophagogastroduodenoscopy. Gut **68**(12), 2161–2169 (2019)
4. Yao, L., et al.: A gastrointestinal endoscopy quality control system incorporated with deep learning improved endoscopist performance in a pretest and post-test trial. Clin. Transl. Gastroenterology **12**(6) (2021)
5. East, J.E., et al.: Advanced endoscopic imaging: European Society of Gastrointestinal Endoscopy (ESGE) technology review. Endoscopy **48**(11), 1029–1045 (2016)
6. Mahmood, F., Chen, R., Durr, N.J.: Unsupervised reverse domain adaptation for synthetic medical images via adversarial training. IEEE Trans. Med. Imaging **37**(12), 2572–2581 (2018)
7. Ganin, Y., Lempitsky V.: Unsupervised domain adaptation by backpropagation. In: International Conference on Machine Learning, pp. 1180–1189. PMLR (2015)
8. Wang, M., Deng, W.: Deep visual domain adaptation: a survey. Neurocomputing **312**, 135–153 (2018)
9. Tzeng, E., et al.: Simultaneous deep transfer across domains and tasks. In: Proceedings of the IEEE International Conference on Computer Vision, pp. 4068–4076 (2015)
10. Li, Y., et al.: Revisiting batch normalization for practical domain adaptation. arXiv preprint arXiv:1603.04779(2016)
11. Liu, M.Y., Tuzel O.: Coupled generative adversarial networks. In: Advances in Neural Information Processing Systems, pp. 469–477 (2016)
12. Tzeng, E., et al.: Adversarial discriminative domain adaptation. In: Proceedings of the IEEE Conference on Computer Vision and Pattern Recognition, pp. 7167–7176 (2017)
13. Bousmalis, K., et al.: Domain separation networks. In: Advances in Neural Information Processing Systems, pp. 343–351 (2016)
14. Yi, Z., et al.: Dualgan: Unsupervised dual learning for image-to-image translation. In: Proceedings of the IEEE International Conference on Computer Vision, pp. 2849–2857 (2017)
15. Peng, X., et al.: Domain agnostic learning with disentangled representations. In: International Conference on Machine Learning, pp. 5102–5112. PMLR (2019)
16. Paszke, A., et al.: PyTorch: an imperative style, high-performance deep learning library. Adv. Neural. Inf. Process. Syst. **32**, 8026–8037 (2019)
17. Zeng, G., et al.: Semantic consistent unsupervised domain adaptation for cross-modality medical image segmentation. In: International Conference on Medical Image Computing and Computer-Assisted Intervention, pp. 201 210 (2021)
18. Perone, C.S., et al.: Unsupervised domain adaptation for medical imaging segmentation with self-ensembling. Neuroimage **194**, 1–11 (2019)
19. Deng, J., et al.: Imagenet: a large-scale hierarchical image database. In: IEEE Conference on Computer Vision and Pattern Recognition, pp. 248–255. (2009)
20. He, K., Zhang, X., Ren, S., Sun, J.: Deep residual learning for image recognition. In: Proceedings of the IEEE Conference on Computer Vision and Pattern Recognition, pp. 770–778 (2016)
21. Howard, A.G., et al.: Mobilenets: efficient convolutional neural networks for mobile vision applications. arXiv preprint arXiv:1704.04861 (2017)
22. Li, Y., et al.: Adaptive batch normalization for practical domain adaptation. Pattern Recogn. **80**, 109–117 (2018)
23. Wang, Z., Bovik, A.C., Sheikh, H.R., Simoncelli, E.P.: Image quality assessment: from error visibility to structural similarity. IEEE Trans. Image Process. **13**(4), 600–612 (2004)

24. Abdelmoneim, R.S.E., Abdelmoety, A.A., Baddour, N., Salem, P., Metawea, M.: The classification of gastric antral vascular ectasia in cirrhotic patients by Versatile Intelligent Staining Technology. Egyptian Liver J. **12**(1), 1–6 (2022)
25. Kingma, D.P., Ba, J.: Adam: a method for stochastic optimization. arXiv preprint arXiv:1412.6980(2014)

Criss-Cross Attention Based Multi-level Fusion Network for Gastric Intestinal Metaplasia Segmentation

Chu-Min Nien[1], Er-Hsiang Yang[2], Wei-Lun Chang[2], Hsiu-Chi Cheng[2], and Chun-Rong Huang[1(✉)] (iD)

[1] Department of Computer Science and Engineering, National Chung Hsing University, Taichung, Taiwan
w107056002@mail.nchu.edu.tw, crhuang@cs.nchu.edu.tw
[2] Department of Internal Medicine and Institute of Clinical Medicine, National Cheng Kung University Hospital, College of Medicine, National Cheng Kung University, Tainan, Taiwan

Abstract. In this paper, we propose a novel criss-cross attention based multi-level fusion network to segment gastric intestinal metaplasia from narrow-band endoscopic images. Our network is composed of two sub-networks including criss-cross attention based feature fusion encoder and feature activation map guided multi-level decoder. The former one learns representative deep features by imposing attention on features of multiple receptive fields. The latter one segments gastric intestinal metaplasia regions by using the feature activation map scheme to enhance the importance of decoder features and avoid overfitting. As shown in the experimental results, our method outperforms state-of-the-art semantic segmentation methods on a novel challenging endoscopic image dataset. The source code is available at https://github.com/nchucvml/CCA-MFNet.

Keywords: Intestinal metaplasia · Semantic segmentation · Attention

1 Introduction

Gastric intestinal metaplasia (IM) is the major gastric precancerous lesion, and the incidence rate of gastric cancer of patients with IM averages 3.38 patients per 1,000 person-years [1]. Patients with gastric IM have a 6.4 to 9.3-fold risk of gastric cancer in East Asians [19] and have higher risk when observing severe IM. Therefore, detecting the presence and assessing the severity of gastric IM are important to select high-risk population and early detect gastric cancer. The gold standard diagnosis of gastric IM is based on histology [8]. However, multiple biopsies of different gastric sections are invasive and costly, and the procedure could result in bleeding. The processing and histological interpretation of biopsies are also time-consuming.

To reduce the burdens of the histologists and the risk of bleeding, endoscopic grading of gastric IM has been developed to stratify the gastric cancer

© The Author(s), under exclusive license to Springer Nature Switzerland AG 2022
L. Manfredi et al. (Eds.): ISGIE 2022/GRAIL 2022, LNCS 13754, pp. 13–23, 2022.
https://doi.org/10.1007/978-3-031-21083-9_2

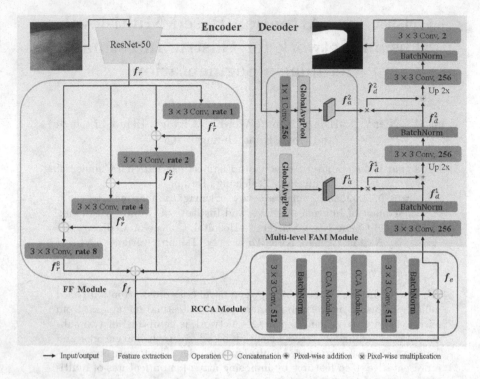

Fig. 1. The overview of the proposed criss-cross attention based multi-level fusion network (CCA-MFNet). The number of filters is 256 if it is not mentioned in the convolutional layer.

risk by using narrow band imaging (NBI) endoscopic images [13,15]. During the endoscopic exam, gastric IM could be missed because of subtle mucosal changes, unclear boundaries and incomplete examination. Moreover, the viewing directions and positions of the endoscopic camera are hard to be consistent for each patient. This situation leads to scale and appearance variations of the captured gastric IM regions. Because of the peristalsis of the stomach, the captured appearances of the mucosa also deform with time. Thus, it is difficult to diagnose gastric IM [2,12] accurately from endoscopic images, and the diagnostic ability of gastric IM heavily depends on the experience of the endoscopists.

To solve the aforementioned problems, we propose a novel criss-cross attention based multi-level fusion network (CCA-MFNet) to achieve gastric IM segmentation from NBI images. As shown in Fig. 1, our network is composed of the criss-cross attention based feature fusion encoder and feature activation map guided multi-level decoder. In the encoder, we propose the feature fusion (FF) module to learn dilated features of different receptive fields. To capture contextual information of the dilated features, the recurrent criss-cross attention [9] (RCCA) module is applied to effectively represent the appearances of the mucosa under scale and deformation changes. In the decoder, we propose the multi-level feature activation map (FAM) module which applies the level context of the layers in the encoder to provide the importance ability to enhance the decoder features and prevent the overfitting. In the experiments, our method outperforms the state-of-the-art methods on the novel challenging dataset.

The contribution of the paper is three-fold. First, to the best of our knowledge, this is the first end-to-end trainable attention based method to achieve gastric IM segmentation from NBI. Second, our method simultaneously aggregates contextual information from different receptive fields based on criss-cross attention to learn novel discriminative features and solve the scale and deformation problems. Third, the novel feature activation map module successfully guides the learning of decoder features to increase the segmentation performance and avoid overfitting.

2   Related Work

Recently, artificial intelligence based methods [11,14,23] have been widely applied to diagnose gastric cancer and polyps from endoscopic images. Compared with these methods, gastric precancerous lesion classification methods can further identify high risk gastric cancer patients [19] before gastric cancer occurs. In white-light imaging (WLI) endoscopic images, Huang et al. [7] propose a refined feature selection based neural network to identify *Helicobacter pylori-induced* gastric IM. Their results are further improved in [6]. Zheng et al. [26] propose using ResNet-50 [5] to identify gastric IM and atrophic gastritis. Instead of using WLI, Yan et al. [24] propose using three different convolutional neural networks for IM classification based on NBI.

Nevertheless, these classification methods have difficulties locating the gastric IM regions which are important to reveal the severity of gastric IM on the mucosa. Wang et al. [21] propose W-Deeplab based on Deeplab-v3 [3] to segment gastric IM regions from WLI. Low-level features of the encoder are concatenated with the features in the decoder without considering the importance of the encoder features. Thus, their decoder features are hard to represent gastric IM. Siripoppohn et al. [18] combine low-level edges and convolutional neural network to achieve gastric IM segmentation. Although they claim the performance is equivalent to Deeplab-v3, their method is not end-to-end trainable. Different from these methods, our criss-cross attention based feature fusion scheme can generate discriminative features in the encoder and our feature activation map scheme can provide the importance for learning decoder features and avoid overfitting in an end-to-end trainable manner from NBI as suggested in [15].

3   Method

3.1   Criss-cross Attention Based Feature Fusion Encoder

In the encoder, we firstly apply the pre-trained ResNet-50 [5] model as the backbone feature extractor. To learn deep features which can represent the appearances of the gastric IM regions under variant scale and deformation changes, the backbone feature f_r is expanded by the feature fusion (FF) module which contains 4 dilated convolutional layers [25] to represent different receptive fields. By using dilated convolutions with different receptive fields, our method can access the multi-scale contextual information of relevant gastric IM regions.

To extend the discriminability of each learned dilated feature, we concatenate f_r with the dilated feature and apply another dilated convolution with a larger dilated rate to generate new dilated features of larger receptive fields. Let f_r^1 be the dilated feature generated by the 3×3 dilated convolution with the dilated rate 1 based on f_r. It is concatenated with f_r and the concatenated feature serves as the input of the next dilated convolutional layer with the larger dilated rate 2 to obtain the dilated feature f_r^2. The same process is repeated for generating the dilated features f_r^4 and f_r^8 of the dilated rates 4 and 8, respectively, as shown in Fig. 1. Such concatenation provides richer representation ability as shown in the ablation study. By aggregating the dilated features of different receptive fields, the fusion feature f_f containing multiple receptive field information of the mucosa is defined as:

$$f_f = [f_r^1 \ f_r^2 \ f_r^4 \ f_r^8]. \tag{1}$$

To further explore the contextual information of f_f, we propose using the recurrent criss-cross attention (RCCA) [9] module by repeating the criss-cross attention (CCA) module twice as shown in Fig. 1. While a single CCA module only captures the contextual information of pixels in horizontal and vertical directions, the RCCA module can represent the contextual information of pixels based on full-image dependencies. To condense f_f, a 3×3 convolutional layer with a batch normalization layer is applied. Then, the first CCA module learns the first attention feature of f_f based on sparse connections of pixels in the same row and the same column which can significantly reduce the number of weights [9] compared with the non-local attention module [22]. To capture the full-image dependencies, the second CCA attention module computes the connections between any two spatial positions of the first attention feature and generates the additional contextual information for all positions. The second attention feature is condensed by using a 3×3 convolutional layer with a batch normalization layer. Finally, the encoder feature f_e is obtained by the concatenation of f_f and the second attention feature.

3.2 Feature Activation Map Guided Multi-level Decoder

To obtain better gastric IM segmentation results of the original resolution in the decoder, a naive idea is to concatenate encoder features with decoder features as U-Net [17] during upsampling. Because of the image scale and deformation variations of captured appearances of the mucosa, the boundaries of the gastric IM regions are hard to be clearly identified. Moreover, different severity of gastric IM also affects the observed region sizes. The learned encoder features can easily overfit the training data. Thus, concatenating encoder features with decoder features is hard for correctly representing the variations of gastric IM.

To solve the aforementioned problems, we propose a novel multi-level feature activation map (FAM) module to improve feature learning during upsampling in the decoder. The multi-level FAM module aims to prevent overfitting and provide the importance of encoder features to enhance decoder features. As shown in [27], the importance can be effectively obtained by using global average pooling on the convolutional features of the encoder. Thus, for the encoder features of the last layer of the residual block, the global average pooling is applied to obtain the feature activation map to represent the importance of the encoder features.

Our decoder contains two level upsampling process as shown in Fig. 1. The encoder feature f_e is passed to a 3×3 convolutional layer with a batch normalization layer to obtain the first decoder feature f_d^1 in the first level. The first feature activation map f_a^1 is obtained by using the global average pooling to the feature of the second residual block in ResNet-50. It then serves as the importance weights and is pixel-wise multiplied to each pixel of f_d^1 of corresponding channels to obtain the importance decoder feature $\hat{f}_d^1$ which reserves key information to avoid overfitting. $\hat{f}_d^1$ is then pixel-wise added to f_d^1 to enhance f_d^1 by considering the importance provided by the encoder. The first enhanced feature is then upsampled and passed to another 3×3 convolutional layer with a batch normalization layer to obtain the second decoder feature f_d^2 in the second level.

The second feature activation map f_a^2 is obtained from the features of the first residual block of ResNet-50 which provides feature importance based on low level features for boundary representation. To reduce the number of channels of the first residual block, a 1×1 convolutional layer is added before the global average pooling to ensure the channel consistency. The same as the process in the first level, f_a^2 is pixel-wise multiplied to f_d^2 and the importance decoder feature $\hat{f}_d^2$ is pixel-wise added to f_d^2. In this way, the encoder features can be used to enhance the decoder feature and avoid overfitting. Finally, a 3×3 convolutional layer, a batch normalization layer, and a 3×3 convolutional layer with the softmax function are applied to compute the cross entropy loss [9] with respect to the gastric IM regions. Please note that the parameters of the ResNet-50 model will also be updated based on the cross entropy loss to help generate better feature activation maps for the decoder.

4   Experimental Results

4.1   Dataset

Patients who underwent gastroscopy (GIF-H290 Endoscope and GIF-H260 Endoscope, Olympus Medical Systems Co., Ltd, Japan) for indications of dyspepsia, acid reflux, melena, gastric intestinal metaplasia or ulcer follow-up and consented to participate the study were enrolled. Patients who took antiplatelet agents or anticoagulants were excluded. In addition, patients with bleeding tendency or hematologic diseases were also excluded. Four endoscopists collected NBI endoscopic images at the lesser and greater curvature of both antrum and corpus, and incisura [16] in every gastroscopy. Invasive biopsies were taken from the above locations to assess gastric IM according to the Updated Sydney System [4]. Two expert gastrointestinal pathologists manually scored the histological grade of gastric IM in each biopsy. The dataset contains NBI images of different gastric sections with various scale changes and viewing directions. The numbers of training and testing images were randomly partitioned to 317 (70%) and 137 (30%), respectively.

For evaluation, we applied mean intersection-over-union (mIoU), mean dice (mDice), recall, precision, and accuracy metrics [9,21]. The NBI images of different gastric locations were extracted and resized to 224×224. Our method was implemented in Pytorch 1.4 on an Intel i7 computer with the GTX 2080 Ti GPU. The batch size was 8 and the up-bound training epochs was 500. The optimizer is the stochastic gradient decent with the learning rate of 0.006, the momentum of 0.7, and the weight decay of 0.0001. The average inference time of the testing images was 0.051 second and the average inference GPU memory usage was 2.6 GB.

Table 1. Ablation study (%).

FAM	FF	RCCA	mIoU	mDice	Recall	Precision	Accuracy
✓	✓		66.93	76.54	73.45	80.79	95.75
✓		✓	66.44	76.07	73.53	79.37	95.56
	✓	✓	65.97	75.54	71.93	80.91	95.69
✓	✓⊖	✓	64.02	73.45	69.76	79.29	95.42
✓	✓	✓	**68.92**	**78.47**	**74.94**	**83.45**	**96.13**

4.2   Ablation Study

Our encoder contains the feature fusion (FF) module and the recurrent crisscross attention (RCCA) module to generate attention features containing rich contextual information from multiple receptive fields. In the decoder, the multilevel feature activation map (FAM) module helps enhance the decoder features and the upsampling process. Table 1 shows the results of the ablation study. Our method achieves the best results when all of the modules are properly applied. In addition, when only aggregating the dilated features in the FF module, the performance will significantly decrease as shown in the fourth row of Table 1. The results show the effectiveness and importance of concatenating the encoder feature with dilated features in the FF module.

4.3   Quantitative Results

In the experiments, we compared the proposed method with the state-of-the-art methods including U-Net [17], U-Net++ [28], nnU-Net [10], MedT [20], W-Deeplab [21], and CCNet [9]. Table 2 shows the quantitative results of the

Table 2. Comparisons with state-of-the-art methods (%).

Method	Backbone	mIoU	mDice	Recall	Precision	Accuracy
U-Net	U-Net	57.61	65.60	61.40	77.18	94.94
U-Net++	U-Net	58.62	66.92	62.55	78.10	95.05
nnU-Net	U-Net	60.33	69.05	64.29	80.47	95.30
MedT	Transformer	53.31	59.44	56.62	71.03	94.46
W-Deeplab	Deeplab-v3	62.19	71.22	65.66	**85.17**	95.69
CCNet	ResNet-50	65.88	75.39	70.80	83.24	95.87
Proposed	ResNet-50	**68.92**	**78.47**	**74.94**	83.45	**96.13**

competing methods and the proposed method with respect to different metrics. Because the viewing directions of the endoscopic camera are not fixed, the distances between the mucosa and the camera will also be variant. Moreover, the deformation of the mucosa also leads to the appearance changes and the gastric IM regions usually do not contain clear boundaries. Thus, the competing methods are hard to achieve good IM segmentation results as shown in Table 2. To solve these problems, we propose attention based feature fusion of multiple receptive fields in the encoder which can successfully represent the contextual information of the gastric IM regions, and the multi-level feature activation maps in the decoder which can enhance the learned features and reduce overfitting for gastric IM segmentation. As a result, the proposed method outperforms all of the competing methods.

4.4 Qualitative Results

Figure 2 shows the qualitative results of the competing methods and the proposed method. The ground truths of gastric IM regions are marked by light green polygons while the segmented gastric IM regions are marked by purple colors. Fig. 2(a) shows the patient ID. The NBI images of patients P1 and P2 contain normal mucosa, while the NBI images of patients P3, P4, P5 and P6 contain gastric IM. As shown in Fig. 2(b) and (c), the false segmentation results of U-Net and U-Net++ can be observed for P1 and P2. respectively. In contrast, the results of nnU-Net for P1 and P2 are better as shown in Fig. 2(d). Due to the lack of multiple receptive field information, these methods fail to segment gastric IM regions of different scales and sizes for remaining patients. Fig. 2(e) shows the segmentation results of MedT. Although MedT can correctly detect normal regions of P1 and P2, miss-segmentation of IM regions can be observed for P4, P5 and P6. When the patient has mild IM, the boundaries of the IM regions are usually unclear which makes it hard to learn the relationship of relative positions by using the transformer.

By imposing encoder features of different receptive fields, W-Deeplab achieves better results but still contains false alarms for normal mucosa of P2, P3 and P6 as shown in Fig. 2(f). It also better segments the IM regions of P4 compared with aforementioned methods. As shown in Fig. 2(g), CCNet achieves better gastric IM segmentation results compared with W-Deeplab, because it extracts representative features based on the attention scheme. Nevertheless, false alarms and miss segmentation of IM regions of P2 and P4 can be observed, when the camera moves close to the mucosa.

In contrast, the proposed method achieves the best qualitative results as shown in Fig. 2(h). It can successfully segment the IM regions of patients with much few false alarms compared with the competing methods. The results show the effectiveness of the three proposed modules. Fig. 2(i) shows the attention maps of the proposed method for each patient. The visualization shows that our method can capture key contextual information to distinguish gastric IM regions and normal regions.

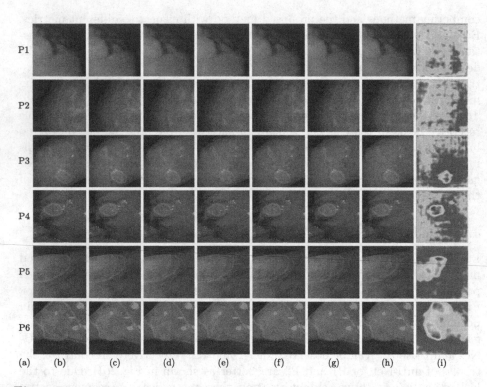

Fig. 2. The qualitative results of the proposed method and the state-of-the-art methods. (a) Patient ID, (b) U-Net, (c) U-Net++, (d) nnU-Net, (e) MedT, (f) W-Deeplab, (g) CCNet, (h) The proposed method, and (i) The attention maps of the proposed method.

5   Conclusions

We propose a novel deep learning network to solve the gastric IM segmentation problem from NBI endoscopic images. By composing the criss-cross attention based feature fusion encoder and the feature activation map guided multi-level decoder, our method can successfully segment gastric IM regions compared with the state-of-the-art methods. With the proposed method, the invasive biopsies can be avoided and the time-consuming histological process can be saved for gastric precancerous lesion diagnosis. In the future, we will append the proposed method to real-time gastroscopy for online gastric IM diagnosis.

Acknowledgements. This work was supported in part by the National Science and Technology Council, Taiwan under Grant MOST 110-2634-F-006-022, 111-2327-B-006-007, and 111-2628-E-005-007-MY3. We would like to thank National Center for High-performance Computing (NCHC) for providing computational and storage resources.

References

1. Akbari, M., Tabrizi, R., Kardeh, S., Lankaran, K.B.: Gastric cancer in patients with gastric atrophy and intestinal metaplasia: a systematic review and meta-analysis. PLoS One **14**(7), e0219865 (2019)
2. An, J.K., et al.: Marginal turbid band and light blue crest, signs observed in magnifying narrow-band imaging endoscopy, are indicative of gastric intestinal metaplasia. BMC Gastroenterol. **12**(169) (2012)
3. Chen, L.C., Papandreou, G., Schroff, F., Adam, H.: Rethinking atrous convolution for semantic image segmentation. CoRR abs/1706.05587 (2017)
4. Dixon, M.F., Genta, R.M., Yardley, J.H., Correa, P.: Classification and grading of gastritis. The updated sydney system. Am. J. Surg. Pathol. **20**(10), 1161–1181 (1996)
5. He, K., Zhang, X., Ren, S., Sun, J.: Deep residual learning for image recognition. In: Proceeding of the Conference Computer Vision and Pattern Recognition, pp. 770–778 (2016)
6. Huang, C.R., Chung, P.C., Sheu, B.S., Kuo, H.J., Popper, M.: Helicobacter pylori-related gastric histology classification using support-vector-machine-based feature selection. IEEE Trans. Inform. Technol. Biomed. **12**(4), 523–531 (2008)
7. Huang, C.R., Sheu, B.S., Chung, P.C., Yang, H.B.: Computerized diagnosis of helicobacter pylori infection and associated gastric inflammation from endoscopic images by refined feature selection using a neural network. Endoscopy **36**(7), 601–608 (2004)
8. Huang, R., Choi, A., Truong, C., Yeh, M., Hwang, J.: Diagnosis and management of gastricintestinal metaplasia: current status and future directions. Gut Liver. **13**(6), 596–603 (2019)
9. Huang, Z., et al.: CCNet: criss-cross attention for semantic segmentation. IEEE Trans. Pattern Anal. Mach. Intell. 1 (2020)
10. Isensee, F., Jaeger, P., Kohl, S., et al.: nnU-Net: a self-configuring method for deep learning-based biomedical image segmentation. Nat. Methods **18**, 203–211 (2021)
11. Kanayama, T., et al.: Gastric cancer detection from endoscopic images using synthesis by GAN. In: Proceedings of the International Conference Medical Image Computing and Computer-Assisted Intervention, pp. 530–538 (2019)

12. Kanemitsu, T., et al.: Extending magnifying NBI diagnosis of intestinal metaplasia in the stomach: the white opaque substance marker. Endoscopy **49**(6), 529–535 (2017)
13. Lin, T.H., et al.: Deep ensemble feature network for gastric section classification. IEEE J. Biomed. Health Inform. **25**(1), 77–87 (2021)
14. Ling, T., et al.: A deep learning-based system for identifying differentiation status and delineating the margins of early gastric cancer in magnifying narrow-band imaging endoscopy. Endoscopy **53**(5), 469–477 (2021)
15. Pimentel-Nunes, P., et al.: A multicenter prospective study of the real-time use of narrow-band imaging in the diagnosis of premalignant gastric conditions and lesions. Endoscopy **48**(8), 723–730 (2016)
16. Pimentel-Nunes, P., et al.: Management of epithelial precancerous conditions and lesions in the stomach (maps ii): european society of gastrointestinal endoscopy (esge), european helicobacter and microbiota study group (ehmsg), european society of pathology (esp), and sociedade portuguesa de endoscopia digestiva (sped) guideline update. Endoscopy **51**(4), 365–388 (2019)
17. Ronneberger, O., Fischer, P., Brox, T.: U-net: convolutional networks for biomedical image segmentation. In: Proceeding of the International Conference Medical Image Computing and Computer-Assisted Intervention, pp. 234–241 (2015)
18. Siripoppohn, V., et al.: Fast segmentation convolutional neural network with edge-guided path for real-time diagnosis of gastric intestinal metaplasia. In: Proceedings of the International Computer Science and Engineering Conference, pp. 200–205 (2021)
19. Uemura et al., N.: Helicobacter pylori infection and the development of gastric cancer. N. Engl. J. Med. **345**(11), 784–789 (2001)
20. Valanarasu, J.M.J., Oza, P., Hacihaliloglu, I., et al.: Medical transformer: gated axial-attention for medical image segmentation. In: Proceedings of the International Conference Medical Image Computing and Computer-Assisted Intervention, pp. 36–46 (2021)
21. Wang, C., Li, Y., Yao, J., Chen, B., Song, J., Yang, X.: Localizing and identifying intestinal metaplasia based on deep learning in oesophagoscope. In: Proceedings of the International Symposium Next Generation Electronics, pp. 1–4 (2019)
22. Wang, X., Girshick, R., Gupta, A., He, K.: Non-local neural networks. In: Proceedings of the Conference Computer Vision and Pattern Recognition, pp. 7794–7803 (2018)
23. Wu, L., Hu, Z., Ji, Y., Luo, P., Zhang, S.: Multi-frame collaboration for effective endoscopic video polyp detection via spatial-temporal feature transformation. In: Proceedings of the International Conference Medical Image Computing and Computer-Assisted Intervention, pp. 302–312 (2021)
24. Yan, T., Wong, P.K., Choi, I.C., Vong, C.M., Yu, H.H.: Intelligent diagnosis of gastric intestinal metaplasia based on convolutional neural network and limited number of endoscopic images. Comput. Biol. Med. **126**, 104026 (2020)
25. Yu, F., Koltun, V.: Multi-scale context aggregation by dilated convolutions. In: Proceedings of the International Conference Learning Representations, pp. 1–13 (2016)
26. Zheng, W., et al.: Deep convolutional neural networks for recognition of atrophic gastritis and intestinal metaplasia based on endoscopy images. Gastrointest. Endosc. **91**, AB533–AB534 (2020)

27. Zhou, B., Khosla, A., Lapedriza, A., Oliva, A., Torralba, A.: Learning deep features for discriminative localization. In: Proceedings of the Conference Computer Vision and Pattern Recognition, pp. 2921–2929 (2016)
28. Zhou, Z., Rahman Siddiquee, M.M., Tajbakhsh, N., Liang, J.: Unet++: a nested u-net architecture for medical image segmentation. In: Deep Learning in Medical Image Analysis and Multimodal Learning for Clinical Decision Support, pp. 3–11 (2018)

Colonoscopy Landmark Detection Using Vision Transformers

Aniruddha Tamhane$^{(\boxtimes)}$, Tse'ela Mida, Erez Posner, and Moshe Bouhnik (iD)

Intuitive Surgical, Inc., 1020 Kifer Road, Sunnyvale, CA, USA
{aniruddha.tamhane,tseela.mida,erez.posner,moshe.bouhnik}@intusurg.com

Abstract. Colonoscopy is a routine outpatient procedure used to examine the colon and rectum for any abnormalities including polyps, diverticula and narrowing of colon structures. A significant amount of the clinician's time is spent in post-processing snapshots taken during the colonoscopy procedure, for maintaining medical records or further investigation. Automating this step can save time and improve the efficiency of the process. In our work, we have collected a dataset of 120 colonoscopy videos and 2416 snapshots taken during the procedure, that have been annotated by experts. Further, we have developed a novel, vision-transformer based landmark detection algorithm that identifies key anatomical landmarks (the appendiceal orifice, ileocecal valve/cecum landmark and rectum retroflexion) from snapshots taken during colonoscopy. Our algorithm uses an adaptive gamma correction during preprocessing to maintain a consistent brightness for all images. We then use a vision transformer as the feature extraction backbone and a fully connected network based classifier head to categorize a given frame into four classes: the three landmarks or a non-landmark frame. We compare the vision transformer (ViT-B/16) backbone with ResNet-101 and ConvNext-B backbones that have been trained similarly. We report an accuracy of 82% with the vision transformer backbone on a test dataset of snapshots.

Keywords: Colonoscopy · Vision transformer · Landmark detection

1 Introduction

Colorectal cancer (CRC) is among the leading causes of death worldwide [4]. In the United States alone, 161,470 individuals are estimated to be diagnosed with CRC and 54,250 individuals are estimated to die from CRC in 2022 [26]. Colorectal cancer incidence rates have been increasing among screening-age individuals aged 65 years and older by 1% per year [27]. Early onset CRC rates have also been on the rise among the patients under the recommended screening age (50 years). Early screening for colorectal abnormalities is associated with a 67% reduction in mortality from CRC [9]. Colonoscopy being the gold standard for CRC screening [13] plays a critical role in mitigating risk.

Snapshots taken during the colonoscopy are a critical yet time-consuming part of the post-procedural diagnosis and documentation. Physicians typically take snapshots of key colon landmarks such as the Appendiceal Orifice (AO), Ileocecal Valve (ICV), Cecum landmark (Cec) and certain findings such as polyps, diverticula, or routine procedural steps such as a Rectum Retroflexion (RecRF), as recommended by the American Gastroenterological Institute [7]. The snapshots are useful in the post-procedural phase to serve as a medical record of the highlights of the colonoscopy and the patient's colonic health or for assessing the extent of the procedure by capturing a snapshot of the appendiceal orifice and ileocecal valve [21].

It has been reported in [19] that a significant amount of a clinician's time is spent maintaining Electronic Health Records. With the increase in demand for colonoscopy procedures, there is a need for improving the efficiency to save the colonoscopy clinician's time. There have been multiple robust, highly accurate and efficient approaches developed for polyp detection [18,23,24]. However, there has been a limited amount of research on landmark detection. To the best of our knowledge, the algorithms developed by [2,16] have been the only attempts at detecting the appendiceal orifice (using classical and deep learning techniques respectively). The deep-learning technique developed by [14] to detect the hepatic and splenic flexure, is the only multi-landmark detection algorithm for colons. We believe that this scarcity of available literature may be due to a lack of availability of expert annotated datasets of colon landmarks and the inherent difficulty of the task due to: *1)* intra-colon (patient) similarity between different regions, *2)* inter-colon (patient) variability in the anatomical structures of the same region of the colon and *3)* non-ideal photometric conditions of the snapshots (due to poor focus, blur, reflections on the colon walls, occlusions by fluids, polyps etc.) Thus, there is a need for developing a robust technique that can accurately identify anatomical landmarks in the colon across multiple patients, that has been rigorously tested on a dataset containing colonoscopy snapshots that are representative of the typical clinical setting. Further, it is important to design a data-efficient training framework that can demonstrably generalize across different anatomies.

We propose a vision transformer based training framework that enables a model trained on videos (which are cheaper to annotate) to be adapted for snapshots. In our work, we address the following problems pertaining our task: *1)* adaptation to differences in data distribution from video-annotations to snapshots *2)* extreme class imbalance, *3)* poor photometric conditions and *4)* inconsistent annotations from experts.

2   Related Work

A large body of work on the application of statistical, physics-based analysis and machine-learning techniques on colonoscopy has accumulated over the years primarily focusing on the detection of polyps and to a lesser extent, colon landmarks. We review the following categories of scientific literature relevant to our work:

2.1   Landmark Detection

Fast, reliable techniques of detecting anatomical landmarks are crucial to medical image analysis. Landmark detection in ultrasound and CT scans is a well explored field, with research on detecting landmarks to utilizing them for organ segmentation [6,11,30,31]. Detecting landmarks in endoscopy and colonoscopy has a smaller yet broader research focusing on identifying different landmarks and regions as a part of the endo-/colonoscopy process. In [2], a shape-based feature extraction model combined with K-Means clustering was used to detect the appendiceal orifice in colonoscopy videos. Since this method relies on edge-based shape detection, there is a possibility of it not working on blurry images, which are characteristic of typical colonoscopy snapshots. A deep-learning based approach was proposed in [1] for detecting the anatomical regions (e.g. stomach, oesophagus etc.) from capsule endoscope frames. This demonstrated the efficacy of deep networks to correctly identify anatomical regions from a single endoscopy frame. The first major attempt at identifying certain colon landmarks from colonoscopy frames using deep neural networks was made by [3]. They trained a large 2D CNN based neural network to classify a given frame as either one of splenic flexure, hepatic flexure or sigmoidal colon junction. Their approach relies on removing blurred frames using a heuristic, and on testing the model on non-overlapping frames from the videos common to the training set.

2.2   Visual Feature Backbones and Optimizers

Convolutional Neural Network based architectures such as the VGG-16 [28] and ResNet101 [12] have traditionally been the most effective and widely used visual feature extraction architectures. The ConvNext [17] is the latest state-of-the-art CNN-based architecture. On the other hand, the transformer architecture [29], which is the standard architecture in Natural Language Processing, has now been adapted for vision-related tasks in [8] showing promising results. Due to the fundamentally different mechanisms of transformer-based (attention) and CNN-based architectures (learned filters), we decide to compare both types of architectures for our task. For our primary model, we use a Vision Transformer pre-trained on the ImageNet dataset as the visual feature extraction backbone. We also independently train a ResNet-101 and a ConvNext based model for comparison. The choice of optimizer used directly affects the optimization landscape impacting the accuracy and ability to generalize, as show in [5]. We use a Sharpness Aware Minimization (SAM) [10] approach to optimizing neural networks due to its positive impact on the accuracy as well as producing semantically meaningful attention maps in case of transformers.

3   Data Collection

We have collected and annotated 120 colonoscopy videos and 2416 snapshots that have been used for training and evaluating our algorithm respectively. We describe the annotation process, training dataset and snapshots dataset in the following subsections.

3.1 Annotations and Cross-Validation

We have annotated the videos on a frame-level and have cross-validated the annotations between the medical experts. This ensures a clinically accurate dataset
that has fine-grain annotations with fewer human errors. We have followed the
same procedure while annotating the training videos as well as the snapshots
dataset. Our annotation methodology is as follows: we separate videos for the
training data (which will be further split into validation and testing sets) and
the snapshots dataset. Separating the data on a video-level is critical to ensure
that the model generalizes well to all the anatomical variations found in colons.
Each of the videos in the training datasets is then labelled on a frame-level by
two medical students independently. Only the frames with a consensus between
the two annotators are chosen for training and the rest are discarded. On the
other hand, each of the videos in the snapshots dataset was examined by a senior
medical expert to extract snapshots, as they would in a clinical setting. Each of
these snapshots was then labelled independently by two senior medical experts,
and a similar consensus-based cross-validation heuristic was used to select the
snapshots with matching annotations from the two experts.

Table 1. Snapshots and test dataset label distribution

Label	Number of frames (Snapshot)	Number of frames (test)
Appendiceal Orifice	518	776
Ileocecal Valve/Cecum Landmark	132	133
Rectum retroflexion	716	140
Other	1050	1488

3.2 Snapshots Dataset

Our snapshots dataset contains 2416 snapshots collected from over 500 videos
(separate from the training pool of 120 videos), identified and annotated by
clinicians as described in Subsect. 3.1. A snapshot is a video frame that contains
the anatomical/procedural feature of interest in reasonable focus, as identified
by a medical specialist in a clinical setting. Each of the snapshots have been
annotated according to the following labels: Appendiceal Orifice (AO), Ileocecal
Valve (ICV)/Cecum Landmark (Cec), Rectum Retroflexion (RecRF) and Other,
which are shown with examples in Fig. 1. Since the Ileocecal Valve and the Cecum
Landmark typically co-occur in snapshots due to their anatomical proximity, we
combine them into a single label. Both of the first two labels describes the
corresponding anatomical landmark. RecRF refers to the procedural action of
retroflexion in the rectum i.e. bending the colonoscope backwards to inspect the
rectum. Any other anatomical finding such as polyps, inflammation or general
anatomical markers have been labelled as "Other". A breakdown of the number
of frames per class has been given in Table 1.

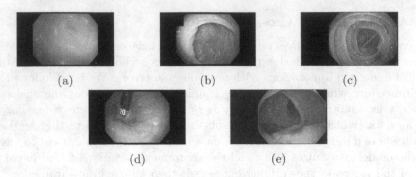

(a)   (b)   (c)

(d)   (e)

Fig. 1. Sample snapshots with following annotations: Appendiceal Orifice (1a), Ileoce-cal Valve (1b), Cecum Landmark (1c), Rectum Retroflexion (1d), Other (1e)

3.3 Training Dataset

Our training dataset has 120 videos constituting of 2,000,000 frames in all, that were annotated and cross-validated as described in Subsect. 3.1. We face an extreme label imbalance, with a majority of frames (>95%) belonging to a non-landmark (Other) class, and the minority containing a landmark of interest. We balance the dataset as part of our training and evaluation (to get a distribution similar to the snapshots dataset) as described in Sect. 6.

4 Problem Definition

We define our problem as follows: identify a function $f : C \times H \times W \to J$ to classify an image frame F as one of the landmark classes $j \in \{\text{AO}, \text{ICV}/\text{Cec},$ $\text{RecRF}, \text{Other}\}$ such that $f(F_{ij}) = j, \quad \forall i \in \mathcal{S}, j \in J$. Here, $\mathcal{S}, J$ denote the set of snapshots and class labels respectively. We approximate f using a deep neural network due to their proven capacity for modeling image data. We thus reduce our problem to finding the optimal weights θ^* for the following empirical loss ($\mathcal{L}$) :

$$\theta^* = \arg\min_{\theta} \sum_{i,j} \mathcal{L}(f(h(F_{ij})|\theta), j) \tag{1}$$

Here, h refers to a general data preprocessing function. Our framework supports any loss function $\mathcal{L}$ that is a distance metric between the predicted probability distribution and the true labels. Based on our experiments, we choose a Kullback-Leibler Divergence [15] as the loss function $\mathcal{L}$.

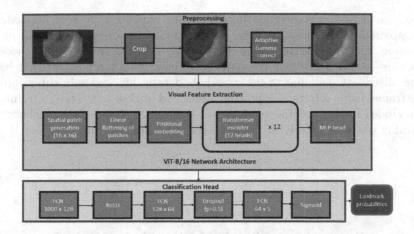

Fig. 2. Landmark detection pipeline architecture

5   Architecture

Our algorithm consists of three primary parts: *1)* image preprocessing, *2)* visual feature extraction and *3)* classification head. The image preprocessing consists of an auto-cropping step to remove dark edges that are an artifact of the colonoscopy software itself, and auto-correct the brightness using gamma correction. Since the brightness varies considerably during a colonoscopy, we use an adaptive gamma correction algorithm described in [25]. We use a pretrained Vision Transformer (ViT-B/16) as the visual feature extraction backbone in our primary model. We also experiment with other CNN based architectures (ResNet101 and ConvNext-B) that were identically pretrained on the ImageNet dataset and benchmark their performances. Finally, we a use a Fully Connected Network (FCN) based classifier head to compute the label probabilities from the feature vector generated by the backbone. A high-level overview of the architecture is given in Fig. 2.

6   Training Pipeline

We design our framework to train a model on annotated videos so that it performs well on clinically selected snapshots. Snapshots are different from video frames because they are hand-picked by clinicians in the following regards: they have a different distribution of landmarks and have a different photometric quality. We address this gap in the training and evaluation data using:

1. *Cross-validation*: Cross-validating frames as explained in Sect. 3.1 reduces the possibility of annotation error and inclusion of poor quality frames in the training. This bridges the gap in data quality between snapshots and videos.
2. *Domain-specific sampling*: We artificially construct a training set that has a label distribution similar to the snapshots dataset by randomly sub-sampling the frames using a Bernoulli process, described in Eqs. 2, 3. Thus, a frame F_{ij} is included in the training set if $Z_{ij} = 1$. Here, $\mathcal{S}$, $\mathcal{T}$ are the snapshots and training sets respectively. $|\Gamma|$ denotes the cardinality of any set Γ.

$$Z_{ij} \sim \text{Bernoulli}(p_j) \tag{2}$$

$$p_j = min\left(\frac{|\bigcup_{i \in \mathcal{S}, k=j} F_{ik}|}{|\bigcup_{i \in \mathcal{S}, k} F_{ik}|} \bigg/ \frac{|\bigcup_{i \in \mathcal{T}, k=j} F_{ik}|}{|\bigcup_{i \in \mathcal{T}, k} F_{ik}|}, 1\right) \tag{3}$$

We repeat the sampling (with replacement) at the beginning of every epoch to maximally cover the downsampled frames.

3. *Sharpness-Aware Minimization Optimizer*: Learning anatomically relevant features and ignoring features generated by varying photometric conditions, specific clinical conditions etc. is critical to generalizability across multiple patient anatomies. We observe that using a SAM optimization scheme as described in [10] for training the neural networks helps learn such a robust model.

7   Results

We have trained Vision Transformer (ViT-B/16), ResNet-101 and ConvNext-B based models using our framework and evaluated the results on our snapshots dataset. We tabulate the corresponding accuracy and the class-wise precision, recall scores in Table 2. We also plot 2D U-MAP [20] embeddings of the vision backbone representations for images from our balanced test dataset in Fig. 3. We report the test dataset statistics in Table 1. We see that the vision transformer based model outperforms the other two on most metrics reported in Table 2. This is also corroborated by the comparatively well-separated clusters in Fig. 3. We believe that the inherent shape bias of vision transformers, as reported in [22], makes it more suitable than CNN-based architectures for landmark detection, since landmarks are reliably identified by their shape regardless of texture.

Table 2. Recall, precision scores and overall accuracy on snapshots dataset

Class	Metric	ViT-B/16 (Main)	ResNet-101	ConvNext-B
Overall	Accuracy	**81.84%**	73.06%	60.45%
AO	Recall	68.15%	69.69%	**75.09%**
	Precision	**76.41%**	55.36%	57.12%
ICV/Cec	Recall	**89.43%**	75.33%	88.11%
	Precision	51.26%	**55.52%**	24.84%
RecRF	Recall	**96.09%**	86.31%	88.12%
	Precision	**98.29%**	97.48%	95.03%
Other	Recall	**77.24%**	65.05%	28.39%
	Precision	**85.10%**	74.48%	82.55%

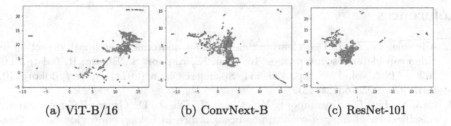

(a) ViT-B/16   (b) ConvNext-B   (c) ResNet-101

Fig. 3. U-MAP embeddings of vision backbone representations with the color scheme: AO (Blue), ICV (Orange), Cec (Green), RecRF (Red), Purple (Other) (Color figure online)

8   Inference and Future Work

We achieve an overall landmark classification accuracy of 81.84% on a snapshot dataset of clinically relevant colon landmarks using a vision transformer backbone. We observe that a transformer based backbone outperforms other state-of-the-art CNN-based backbones such as ResNet-101 and ConvNext-B. We can visually see that well-separated representations on an independent, balanced test set imply a higher accuracy in Fig. 3. This may be due to the transformer's inherently higher shape bias as reported by [22]. We hypothesize thus, since the accuracy trend is not completely explained by the number of parameters, with ViT-B/16 (86.6M) and ConvNext-B (89M) having a comparable number of parameters.

Further, the Rectum Retroflexion class has the highest precision and recall scores as well as the best separation on the U-MAP plots. This is because most RecRF frames are characterized by the presence of a metallic/plastic tube indicating the inversion of the colonoscope head. We further observe that the precision for AO and ICV classes is relatively lower. This is also evidenced by the poorer separation of the corresponding clusters in Fig. 3. This can be explained by the visual similarity between these two landmarks and other parts of the colon (labelled "Other"), making it a challenging task. Thus, we can conclude from our results that detecting subtle anatomical features (such as a cecum landmark) as opposed to specific shapes (such as the retroflexion tube) is challenging for the vision backbone.

Finally, we believe incorporating temporal information in our future work will help remove false positives for both these classes and improve precision. We also believe that more complex training techniques such as active learning, self-supervised pre-training can further improve the quality of features learned by the vision backbone and improve accuracy. So, we plan on incorporating them in our future pipeline. We also plan on including more landmark classes such as polyps and diverticula in the future.

References

1. Adewole, So., et al.: Deep learning methods for anatomical landmark detection in video capsule endoscopy images. In: Arai, K., Kapoor, S., Bhatia, R. (eds.) FTC 2020. AISC, vol. 1288, pp. 426–434. Springer, Cham (2021). https://doi.org/10.1007/978-3-030-63128-4_32
2. Cao, Y., Liu, D., Tavanapong, W., Wong, J., Oh, J., De Groen, P.C.: Automatic classification of images with appendiceal orifice in colonoscopy videos. In: 2006 International Conference of the IEEE Engineering in Medicine and Biology Society, pp. 2349–2352. IEEE (2006)
3. Che, K., et al.: Deep learning-based biological anatomical landmark detection in colonoscopy videos. arXiv preprint arXiv:2108.02948 (2021)
4. Chen, J., et al.: Cause of death among patients with colorectal cancer: a population-based study in the united states. Aging (Albany NY) **12**(22), 22927 (2020)
5. Chen, X., Hsieh, C.J., Gong, B.: When vision transformers outperform resnets without pretraining or strong data augmentations. arXiv preprint arXiv:2106.01548 (2021)
6. Chowdhury, A.S., Yao, J., VanUitert, R., Linguraru, M.G., Summers, R.M.: Detection of anatomical landmarks in human colon from computed tomographic colonography images. In: 2008 19th International Conference on Pattern Recognition, pp. 1–4. IEEE (2008)
7. Cooper, J.A., Ryan, R., Parsons, N., Stinton, C., Marshall, T., Taylor-Phillips, S.: The use of electronic healthcare records for colorectal cancer screening referral decisions and risk prediction model development. BMC Gastroenterol. **20**(1), 1–16 (2020)
8. Dosovitskiy, A., et al.: An image is worth 16x16 words: transformers for image recognition at scale. arXiv preprint arXiv:2010.11929 (2020)
9. Doubeni, C.A., et al.: Effectiveness of screening colonoscopy in reducing the risk of death from right and left colon cancer: a large community-based study. Gut **67**(2), 291–298 (2018). https://doi.org/10.1136/gutjnl-2016-312712, https://gut.bmj.com/content/67/2/291
10. Foret, P., Kleiner, A., Mobahi, H., Neyshabur, B.: Sharpness-aware minimization for efficiently improving generalization. arXiv preprint arXiv:2010.01412 (2020)

11. Ghesu, F.C., Georgescu, B., Mansi, T., Neumann, D., Hornegger, J., Comaniciu, D.: An artificial agent for anatomical landmark detection in medical images. In: Ourselin, S., Joskowicz, L., Sabuncu, M.R., Unal, G., Wells, W. (eds.) MICCAI 2016. LNCS, vol. 9902, pp. 229–237. Springer, Cham (2016). https://doi.org/10.1007/978-3-319-46726-9_27
12. He, K., Zhang, X., Ren, S., Sun, J.: Deep residual learning for image recognition. In: Proceedings of the IEEE Conference on Computer Vision and Pattern Recognition, pp. 770–778 (2016)
13. Issa, I.A., Noureddine, M.: Colorectal cancer screening: an updated review of the available options. World J. Gastroenterol. 23(28), 5086 (2017)
14. Jheng, Y.C., et al.: A novel machine learning-based algorithm to identify and classify lesions and anatomical landmarks in colonoscopy images. Surg. Endoscopy 1–11 (2021)
15. Kim, T., Oh, J., Kim, N., Cho, S., Yun, S.Y.: Comparing kullback-leibler divergence and mean squared error loss in knowledge distillation. arXiv preprint arXiv:2105.08919 (2021)
16. Lebedev, A., Khryashchev, V., Kazina, E., Zhuravleva, A., Kashin, S., Zavyalov, D.: Automatic identification of appendiceal orifice on colonoscopy images using deep neural network. In: 2020 IEEE East-West Design & Test Symposium (EWDTS), pp. 1–5. IEEE (2020)
17. Liu, Z., Mao, H., Wu, C.Y., Feichtenhofer, C., Darrell, T., Xie, S.: A convnet for the 2020s. arXiv preprint arXiv:2201.03545 (2022)
18. Mamonov, A.V., Figueiredo, I.N., Figueiredo, P.N., Tsai, Y.H.R.: Automated polyp detection in colon capsule endoscopy. IEEE Trans. Med. Imaging 33(7), 1488–1502 (2014)
19. McDonald, C.J., Callaghan, F.M., Weissman, A., Goodwin, R.M., Mundkur, M., Kuhn, T.: Use of internist's free time by ambulatory care electronic medical record systems. JAMA Internal Med. 174(11), 1860–1863 (2014)
20. McInnes, L., Healy, J., Melville, J.: Umap: uniform manifold approximation and projection for dimension reduction. arXiv preprint arXiv:1802.03426 (2018)
21. Morelli, M.S., Miller, J.S., Imperiale, T.F.: Colonoscopy performance in a large private practice: a comparison to quality benchmarks. J. Clin. Gastroenterol. 44(2), 152–153 (2010)
22. Morrison, K., Gilby, B., Lipchak, C., Mattioli, A., Kovashka, A.: Exploring corruption robustness: inductive biases in vision transformers and mlp-mixers. arXiv preprint arXiv:2106.13122 (2021)
23. Park, S.Y., Sargent, D., Spofford, I., Vosburgh, K.G., Yousif, A., et al.: A colon video analysis framework for polyp detection. IEEE Trans. Biomed. Eng. 59(5), 1408–1418 (2012)
24. Qadir, H.A., Shin, Y., Solhusvik, J., Bergsland, J., Aabakken, L., Balasingham, I.: Toward real-time polyp detection using fully CNNS for 2d gaussian shapes prediction. Med. Image Anal. 68, 101897 (2021)
25. Rahman, S., Rahman, M.M., Abdullah-Al-Wadud, M., Al-Quaderi, G.D., Shoyaib, M.: An adaptive gamma correction for image enhancement. EURASIP J. Image Video Process. 2016(1), 1–13 (2016). https://doi.org/10.1186/s13640-016-0138-1
26. Siegel, R.L., Miller, K.D., Fuchs, H.E., Jemal, A.: Cancer statistics, 2022. CA: A Cancer J. Clin. 72, 7–33 (2022)
27. Siegel, R.L., et al.: Colorectal cancer statistics, 2020. CA: A Cancer J. Clin. 70(3), 145–164 (2020)
28. Simonyan, K., Zisserman, A.: Very deep convolutional networks for large-scale image recognition. arXiv preprint arXiv:1409.1556 (2014)

29. Vaswani, A., et al.: Attention is all you need. In: Advances in Neural Information Processing Systems, pp. 5998–6008 (2017)
30. Zhou, S.K., et al.: A review of deep learning in medical imaging: Imaging traits, technology trends, case studies with progress highlights, and future promises. In: Proceedings of the IEEE (2021)
31. Zhou, S.K., Xu, Z.: Landmark detection and multiorgan segmentation: representations and supervised approaches. In: Handbook of Medical Image Computing and Computer Assisted Intervention, pp. 205–229. Elsevier (2020)

Real-Time Lumen Detection
for Autonomous Colonoscopy

Baidaa Al-Bander[1], Alwyn Mathew[1], Ludovic Magerand[2], Emanuele Trucco[2],
and Luigi Manfredi[1(✉)]

[1] School of Medicine, University of Dundee, Dundee, UK
l.manfredi@dundee.ac.uk
[2] School of Science and Engineering, University of Dundee, Dundee, UK

Abstract. Lumen detection and tracking in the large bowel is a key pre-requisite step for autonomous navigation of endorobots for colonoscopy. Attempts at detecting and tracking the lumen so far have been made using optical flow and shape-from-shading techniques. In general, these methods are computationally expensive, and most are either not real-time nor tested on real devices. To this end, we present a deep learning-based approach for lumen localisation from colonoscopy videos. We avoid the need for extensive, costly annotations with a semi-supervised learning and a self-training scheme, whereby only a small subset of video frames is annotated. We develop an end-to-end pseudo-labelling semi-supervised approach incorporating a self-training scheme for colon lumen detection. Our approach reveals a competitive performance to the supervised baseline model with both objective and subjective evaluation metrics, while saving heavy labelling costs in terms of clinicians' time. Our method for lumen detection runs at 60 ms per frame during the inference phase. Our experiments demonstrate the potential of our system in real-time environments, which contributes towards improving the automation of robotics colonoscopy.

Keywords: Autonomous colonoscopy · Semi-supervised learning · Lumen detection · Self-training · Endorobots for colonoscopy · Bowel cancer

1 Introduction

Colorectal cancer (CRC) is the third cause of cancer-related mortality worldwide, after lung and breast cancer [1]. Colonoscopy is regarded as the main clinical diagnostic technique for CRC, with regular screening being a significant step in drastically reducing mortality rates. Optical colonoscopy (OC) is the gold standard for optical screening and treatment of CRC since it enables biopsy, pathological prediction and treatment [5]. However, the current generation of colonoscopes has limitations, such as patient pain and discomfort, narrow field of view, difficulties to detect lesions located behind colonic folds, time-consuming

L. Manfredi et al. (Eds.): ISGIE 2022/GRAIL 2022, LNCS 13754, pp. 35–44, 2022.
https://doi.org/10.1007/978-3-031-21083-9_4

and complex procedure to learn [16]. Thus, developing low-risk, cost-effective, and more efficient alternative solutions for colonoscopy is now necessary. Rapid advancements in endorobotics have produced a new generation of systems that have the potential to overcome the above limitations. For instance, real-time visual feedback from a monocular camera can now be incorporated into the control loop to detect the region of haustral folds in the colon and determine the centre of the lumen [14,15]. The deformable nature of the large bowel poses sensing and navigation challenges untackled by traditional robotics. Current localisation and navigation strategies for colonoscopy [8] generally depend on external hardware (i.e. permanent on-board magnet linked to an external magnetic field). Computer vision-based navigation and localisation, relying on feature recognition, can offer a solution, but, the deformable nature of the environment may cause significant difficulties to traditional feature location methods [21].

Several approaches to designing autonomous visual navigation systems for endoscopes using images have been reported [24]. Many are unsuitable for real-time operation or fail to work when the lumen centre is hard to detect. Despite these challenges, methods based on optical flow [11], shape from shading [6], structure from motion [10] and segmentation [17] have been developed for automatic navigation. The considerable variety in lumen feature appearance due to the surfaces in view, lighting and acquisition techniques makes it challenging to construct a universal model performing optimally in any environment and condition. In addition, further factors like occlusion, deformation, off-centre lumen can degrade performance. Deep learning (DL) algorithms offer great potential in medical image analysis and interpretation, supported by rapid improvements in GPU hardware. Endoscopists' performance in the diagnosis of adenoma or polyp [4] has also been shown to benefit from the assistance of deep learning systems. Ahmad et al. [2] reported a comprehensive review of studies that exploited artificial intelligence, especially DL models, in colonoscopy computer-aided diagnosis. Methods based on supervised learning (SL) typically require large quantities of labelled data annotated by experts to achieve high diagnostic accuracy. However, in the medical domain, only a limited amount of labelled data and a considerably greater amount of unlabelled data is available. Contrary to SL, semi-supervised learning (SSL) leverages both labelled and unlabelled data to offer a low-cost alternative to the time-consuming massive data labelling task [12,20,23,25,27,28].

Our work develops a vision-based system harnessing deep neural networks to detect and track the lumen in real time, enabling reliable endorobot navigation colonoscopy. Unlike existing lumen detection models developed to work on specific video data, our model is developed to accommodate video data captured from a variety of environments, including synthetic, plastic phantom, and real colonoscopy videos. We introduce a fast and accurate method that controls the level of supervision needed, leveraging a semi-supervised scheme for lumen localisation. By exploiting a few labelled frames and a large number of unlabelled frames, we develop an end-to-end pseudo-labelling semi-supervised approach incorporating a self-training scheme for colon lumen detection. To evaluate robustness and reliability, we have conducted experiments on comprehensive video data. Results show promising recall and precision on lumen detection with plastic phantom and simulated datasets and suggest an excellent generalisation ability on unseen real colonoscopy videos. The results also demonstrate the benefits of the SSL strategy over the fully supervised scheme (baseline model), without sacrificing the run-time advantage or prediction accuracy.

2   Methods

Inspired by Xu et al. [27], who achieved competitive detection performance on natural image data, we propose to use a semi-supervised learning (SSL) scheme incorporating a self-training framework for colon lumen detection, as shown in Fig. 1. Our method exploits the mentor-student approach for a hybrid learning strategy. Both mentor and student have the same architecture, the default Faster R-CNN object detector model. First, the object detector model is trained with a classical supervised scheme from 40% of the labelled data, of which 2% are used for validation and hyper-parameters tuning. The object detector is then used as a mentor to generate pseudo-labels, as a test-time inference, from 30% of unlabelled data. The student is trained by mixing those pseudo-labelled data with an additional 10% of the labelled data, which is augmented. The remaining 20% of labelled data are used for testing.

Baseline Supervised object Detector Model. A single-level feature detector, Faster Region Based Convolutional Neural Networks (Faster R-CNN) [19] is harnessed to produce the baseline model used as mentor in our SSL scheme. We trained it with a classical supervised scheme using 40% of the manually labelled

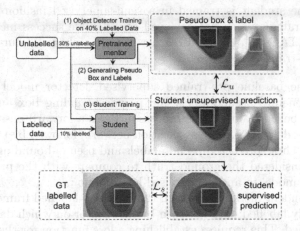

Fig. 1. Overview of mentor-student model training for lumen detection. Pseudo-labels (bounding boxes and class labels) are generated from a pre-trained mentor model with unlabelled data. Student unsupervised loss is computed with the pseudo-labels above a specific threshold in a semi-supervised manner. 10% of the labelled data with augmentation is also used to train the student model. GT: ground truth.

frames. Faster R-CNN has two heads, one for object classification and the other for bounding boxes regression. It also has a fully convolutional Region Proposal Network (RPN) that takes the input features of frame and produces region proposals with an objectness score (denoting the probability of object or not object (background) for each proposal). The RPN predicts the offsets of region proposals from established reference boxes, known as anchor boxes. Anchor boxes are predetermined and fixed-size boxes distributed over the input frame with a variety of sizes and aspect ratios. A non-maximum suppression (NMS) algorithm [9] is then applied to filter out the predicted region proposals, depending on a confidence threshold score, which is set to value of 0.7. The advantage of employing box predictions after NMS over raw predictions (before applying NMS) is that it avoids duplicated and overlapped results. Once the region proposals are selected, the lumen object classification and boundary box regression are then measured in a supervised fashion. The supervised loss function used to learn the baseline model is:

$$\mathcal{L}_s = \frac{1}{N_l} \sum_{i=1}^{N_l} \left(\mathcal{L}_{cls}\left(p_i, p_i^* \right) + \mathcal{L}_{reg}\left(t_i, t_i^* \right) \right) \tag{1}$$

where i indexes a labelled frame, p_i: predicted probability of proposal contains a lumen object or not, p_i^*: the ground-truth value of proposal contains a lumen object or not, t_i is the coordinates of the predicted lumen proposal, t_i^* is the ground-truth coordinate associated with the bounding box of the lumen, $\mathcal{L}_{cls}$ is the classification loss, $\mathcal{L}_{reg}$ is the bounding box regression loss, and N_l denotes the number of labelled frames in batch.

Semi-supervised with Self-training Model. In our mentor-student learning scheme, the student is trained in a semi-supervised fashion integrating a self-training strategy which has achieved considerable success including Noise-Student [26], STAC [23], and SoftTeacher [27]. The phases of our SSL incorporated with self-training are:

1. Leverage the baseline pre-trained supervised detector model as a mentor model to generate pseudo-labels and pseudo-bounding box annotations for 30% of unlabelled frames. This process includes a forward pass of the Res50 backbone model, RPN and classification network, followed by the NMS postprocessing. These predicted pseudo-labels and pseudo-bounding box annotations are considered the ground truth to compare with the prediction from the student model in an unsupervised loss function.
2. Train the student model using both those pseudo-labelled frames and 10% of the manually labelled data not seen by the mentor on which data augmentation is applied. This requires establishing a loss function for the student that sums the losses of both supervised and unsupervised models.

To compute the loss for pseudo-labelled frames when training the student, the generated pseudo-labels are used as ground-truth to be compared to the student prediction, producing an unsupervised loss function as follows:

$$\mathcal{L}_u = \frac{1}{N_u} \sum_{i=1}^{N_u} \left(\mathcal{L}_{\text{cls}}\left(r_i, r_i^*\right) + \mathcal{L}_{\text{reg}}\left(s_i, s_i^*\right) \right) \tag{2}$$

Here i indexes an unlabelled frame, u an unlabelled frame, r_i refers to the predicted probability of proposal containing a lumen object, r_i^* represents the generated pseudo-label of proposal, s_i is the coordinates of predicted proposal for lumen, s_i^* is the pseudo-boxes of lumen generated by the mentor, N_u denotes the number of unlabelled frames. For the 10% labelled frames, the student calculates the loss between the provided ground truth and the predicted labels, via a supervised loss. The total loss of the student model is the weighted sum of the unsupervised and supervised losses, i.e., using Eq. (1) and Eq. (2):

$$\mathcal{L} = \mathcal{L}_s + \alpha \mathcal{L}_u \tag{3}$$

where α denotes the weight of unsupervised loss, determined experimentally.

Inference and Refinement. Once the model is trained, it can be adopted for the inference phase to produce the predictions of bounding boxes over the lumen area on a frame basis. To maintain the temporal consistency among predicted bounding boxes on a sequence of consecutive frames, we carefully designed a simple yet effective strategy to choose the bounding box proposal that preserves a minimum distance to the bounding box in the previous frame in a sequence of frames. The application of refinement scheme assumes that the intersection over the union between the bounding boxes of two consecutive frames is not null, which typically results from an abrupt camera movement. This scheme is applied by locating the centre points $(x_{i,c}, y_{i,c})$ of the predicted bounding boxes in frame i, where $c \geq 1$. The centre points are computed from the predicted bounding boxes, represented by the value of top left corner (x_{min}, y_{min}) and bottom right corner (x_{max}, y_{max}). The centre point (x_c, y_c) in frame i is defined as follows:

$$(x_c, y_c) = (round(x_{min} + \frac{x_{max} - x_{min}}{2}), round(y_{min} + \frac{y_{max} - y_{min}}{2})) \tag{4}$$

Euclidean distance is measured among the centre points in frame i and the centre point in the previous frame, $i - 1$. The centre point that achieves the minimum distance is then selected, and the bounding box accompanied by this point is produced as the outcome of the model prediction.

3   Experimental Set-Up, Results and Discussion

Datasets. Public synthetic dataset [18] consisting of 16,016 RGB frames generated from the video is used in our study. The size of frames is 256×256 pixels. The synthetic dataset is split into groups according to texture and lighting conditions. The synthetic dataset collection setting is available in [18]. To obtain the ground truth bounding boxes of the lumen, we used the ground truth depth data provided the synthetic dataset. The depth map is clipped at 3/4 depth from the nearest depth value to segment the lumen. The result is then converted to rectangular bounding boxes. The second set of videos used in our study was acquired with a plastic phantom, an off-the-shelf full HD camera (MISUMI SYT, 1920×1080, 30 Hz, field of view of $140°$) and a colon model used for training medical professionals. The model is made from plastic and mimics 1-to-1 the anatomy of the human colon, including internal diameter, and overall length haustral folds (small, segmented pouches of the bowel) to yield accurately simulated images from an optical colonoscope. Creating the haustral folds with this model does not require inflation with air. The camera is connected to a shaft used to navigate inside the plastic colon-rectum tube forward and backward. The external diameter of the camera is 7 mm, including light illumination and lens. The number of frames generated from plastic phantom video is 2,042. The annotations of labelled frames in this dataset have been conducted manually using LabelImg[1] software by drawing the bounding boxes around the lumen.

DL Experimental Settings. We used Faster R-CNN [19] as a fully supervised baseline algorithm in our experiments. Our model and baseline model were trained for 32,000 iterations on plastic phantom data, and for 52,000 iterations on synthetic data as the size of video data varies. The size of the batch was set to 8 with stochastic gradient descent SGD with an initial learning rate of 10^{-2} with momentum 0.9 and weight decay 10^{-3}, which decays by dividing by 10 at iterations 36,000 and 48,000 on synthetic data and 18000 and 28,000 iterations on plastic phantom frames. We also set the unsupervised weight to $\alpha = 2$. The confidence threshold score is set to 0.8 in the inference phase. The models are implemented using Pytorch and trained on an Nvidia RTX A6000 GPU with a memory of 48 GB. The implementation of Faster R-CNN with Res50 and hyper-parameter setting are based on the MMDetection library [3]. For data augmentation, we follows the same augmentation schemes applied in FixMatch [22] including colour transformations, translation with translation ratio of $(0, 0.1)$, rotation with angle $(0, 30)$, shifting with angle $(0, 30)$, cut-out [7] with ratio $(0.05, 0.2)$ and number of regions $[1, 5]$.

Results. We evaluated the lumen detection model using both quantitative and qualitative measurements. In terms of qualitative evaluation, we summarise in Fig. 2 a comparison of the semi-supervised model against the baseline model on both video types. For quantitative analysis, shown in Table 1, we use the typical object detection metrics, including average precision (AP) and average recall (AR) using various Intersection over Union (IoU) threshold scores. Although the semi-supervised model was trained on only 10% of frames, it shows a competitive performance without needing expensive manual annotations. Importantly, our lumen detection runs in 60 ms including post-processing time, meeting interventional time requirements.

Discussion. The non-learning based methods [6,10,11,17] have not reported evaluation performance compared to ground truth in overlapping with the bounding boxes. Recently, authors in [29] used off-the-shelf fully supervised

---

[1] https://github.com/tzutalin/labelImg.

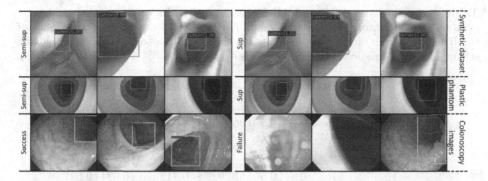

Fig. 2. The qualitative results of lumen detection on test data of synthetic dataset and plastic phantom, respectively. It can be observed that semi-supervised (Semi-sup in figure) prediction accuracy is par with the fully supervised (Sup in figure) model prediction on both datasets. Success and failure cases of the proposed model on real colonoscopy images. Light scattering and low illumination in very challenging conditions are found to affect the prediction.

model Yolo3 to localise the lumen targeting to develop semi-automated navigation. They reported an AP of 0.835 with an IoU threshold score of 0.7 achieved by a model trained on 7,147 fully labelled frames captured from plastic phantom. In contrast, the size of our plastic phantom data was only 2,042 frames in total. To further evaluate the generalisation ability, robustness and reliability of the presented model, three colonoscopy videos taken from publicly available dataset [13] that contain a variety of polyps and complex bowel environments are tested on the developed semi-supervised model, pre-trained on the plastic phantom video data. The obtained detection results shown in Fig. 2 (third row) reveal superior performance on unseen real colonoscopy data. Due to the lack of ground truth bounding boxes of these datasets, the lumen detection results on the real colonoscopy videos have been examined by an anonymous survey involving eight senior clinicians. Purpose of this study was to have a qualitative evaluation on the accuracy of the lumen detection. We established a questionnaire showing a rating scale in range (1 - Extremely poor, 5 - Excellent). The average accuracy reported by the clinicians was 4.37 out of 5. These findings demonstrate that the proposed deep feature learning-based approach will be a valuable automated navigation tool to be deployed in a challenging real-time environment during robotics colonoscopy. Furthermore, the integration of automated systems based on large unlabelled data will also significantly reduce the manual data annotations workload and thus reduce costs. Our proposed model has limitations. The real scenario may be more challenging when a colon has an abnormality, such as big polyps, cancer, and diverticula. We target in our future work to systematically study all scenarios, investigate how the model could cope with various conditions and include more ablation studies for experimental settings. More experiments on both two-stage and one-stage detectors will be also conducted to study the generalisation of this method.

Table 1. Comparison of AP and AR for supervised and semi-supervised models on synthetic and phantom data, at different IoU threshold scores. The performance of the Res50 backbone model is also explored here. In addition to the 10% data splitting scheme, the performance of the SSL model is examined in a 5% data splitting scenario.

Data	Split	Backbone	IoU	Semi-supervised		Supervised	
				AP	AR	AP	AR
Synthetic	10%	Res50	0.5–0.95	0.637	0.633	0.621	0.674
			0.5	0.989	0.688	0.978	0.674
			0.75	0.763	0.688	0.713	0.674
		Res101	0.5–0.95	0.668	0.718	0.624	0.691
			0.5	0.989	0.715	0.978	0.681
			0.75	0.807	0.700	0.728	0.689
	5%	Res50	0.5–0.95	0.601	0.662	0.602	0.655
			0.5	0.977	0.667	0.977	0.649
			0.75	0.703	0.669	0.700	0.660
		Res101	0.5–0.95	0.634	0.691	0.616	0.680
			0.5	0.988	0.680	0.976	0.682
			0.75	0.753	0.694	0.700	0.689
Phantom	10%	Res50	0.5–0.95	0.572	0.651	0.562	0.640
			0.5	0.936	0.651	0.950	0.640
			0.75	0.677	0.651	0.638	0.640
		Res101	0.5–0.95	0.567	0.652	0.554	0.632
			0.5	0.933	0.662	0.960	0.637
			0.75	0.628	0.658	0.613	0.632
	5%	Res50	0.5–0.95	0.518	0.600	0.497	0.603
			0.5	0.948	0.604	0.925	0.609
			0.75	0.521	0.600	0.478	0.606
		Res101	0.5–0.95	0.470	0.570	0.452	0.544
			0.5	0.896	0.559	0.950	0.540
			0.75	0.441	0.560	0.325	0.556

4   Conclusions

In this paper, a novel real-time lumen detection and tracking method has been introduced and tested in a plastic phantom, synthetic and real colonoscopy videos. We have introduced the SSL approach toward real-time bound boxes detection of the lumen, allowing for autonomous navigation and thus providing significant benefits in terms of reduced physical burden and demanding the minimum intervention from the operator. Our findings support our key claim that a reliable medical AI-based solution could be established using a small quantity of labelled data combined with other unlabelled data. A paradigm shift like this might pave the way for intelligent robot-assisted diagnosis and treatment.

Acknowledgements. This work was supported by the UK Engineering and Physical Sciences Research Council (EPSRC) grant number EP/W00433X/1.

References

1. Global cancer statistics 2020: Globocan estimates of incidence and mortality worldwide for 36 cancers in 185 countries. https://acsjournals.onlinelibrary.wiley.com/doi/full/10.3322/caac.21660. Accessed 27 Feb 2022
2. Ahmad, O.F., et al.: Artificial intelligence and computer-aided diagnosis in colonoscopy: current evidence and future directions. Lancet Gastroenterol. Hepatol. **4**(1), 71–80 (2019). https://doi.org/10.1016/S2468-1253(18)30282-6
3. Chen, K., et al.: Mmdetection: Open mmlab detection toolbox and benchmark. arXiv preprint arXiv:1906.07155 (2019)
4. Chen, P.J., Lin, M.C., Lai, M.J., Lin, J.C., Lu, H.H.S., Tseng, V.S.: Accurate classification of diminutive colorectal polyps using computer-aided analysis. Gastroenterology **154**(3), 568–575 (2018). https://doi.org/10.1053/j.gastro.2017.10.010
5. Citarda, F., et al.: Efficacy in standard clinical practice of colonoscopic polypectomy in reducing colorectal cancer incidence. Gut **48**(6), 812–815 (2001). https://doi.org/10.1136/gut.48.6.812
6. Ciuti, G., Visentini-Scarzanella, M., Dore, A., Menciassi, A., Dario, P., Yang, G.Z.: Intra-operative monocular 3d reconstruction for image-guided navigation in active locomotion capsule endoscopy. In: 2012 4th IEEE RAS & EMBS International Conference on Biomedical Robotics and Biomechatronics (BioRob), pp. 768–774. IEEE (2012). https://doi.org/10.1109/BioRob.2012.6290771
7. DeVries, T., Taylor, G.W.: Improved regularization of convolutional neural networks with cutout. arXiv preprint arXiv:1708.04552 (2017)
8. Di Natali, C., Beccani, M., Valdastri, P.: Real-time pose detection for magnetic medical devices. IEEE Trans. Magn. **49**(7), 3524–3527 (2013). https://doi.org/10.1109/TMAG.2013.2240899
9. Girshick, R., Donahue, J., Darrell, T., Malik, J.: Rich feature hierarchies for accurate object detection and semantic segmentation. In: Proceedings of the IEEE Conference on Computer Vision and Pattern Recognition, pp. 580–587 (2014). https://doi.org/10.1109/CVPR.2014.81
10. Lamarca, J., Parashar, S., Bartoli, A., Montiel, J.M.M.: Defslam: tracking and mapping of deforming scenes from monocular sequences. IEEE Trans. Rob. **37**(1), 291–303 (2021). https://doi.org/10.1109/TRO.2020.3020739
11. Liu, J., Subramanian, K.R., Yoo, T.S.: An optical flow approach to tracking colonoscopy video. Comput. Med. Imaging Graph. **37**(3), 207–223 (2013). https://doi.org/10.1016/j.compmedimag.2013.01.010
12. Liu, Q., Yu, L., Luo, L., Dou, Q., Heng, P.A.: Semi-supervised medical image classification with relation-driven self-ensembling model. IEEE Trans. Med. Imaging **39**(11), 3429–3440 (2020)
13. Ma, Y., Chen, X., Cheng, K., Li, Y., Sun, B.: LDPolypVideo benchmark: a large-scale colonoscopy video dataset of diverse polyps. In: de Bruijne, M., Cattin, P.C., Cotin, S., Padoy, N., Speidel, S., Zheng, Y., Essert, C. (eds.) MICCAI 2021. LNCS, vol. 12905, pp. 387–396. Springer, Cham (2021). https://doi.org/10.1007/978-3-030-87240-3_37

14. Manfredi, L.: Endorobots for colonoscopy: design challenges and available technologies. Frontiers in Robotics and AI, p. 209 (2021). https://doi.org/10.3389/frobt.2021.705454
15. Manfredi, L., Capoccia, E., Ciuti, G., Cuschieri, A.: A soft pneumatic inchworm double balloon (spid) for colonoscopy. Sci. Rep. **9**(1), 1–9 (2019). https://doi.org/10.1038/s41598-019-47320-3
16. Miguel, M.N., et al.: Capsule endoscopy versus colonoscopy for the detection of polyps and cancers. Cancéro Digest (2009)
17. Prendergast, J.M., Formosa, G.A., Heckman, C.R., Rentschler, M.E.: Autonomous localization, navigation and haustral fold detection for robotic endoscopy. In: 2018 IEEE/RSJ International Conference on Intelligent Robots and Systems (IROS), pp. 783–790. IEEE (2018). https://doi.org/10.1109/IROS.2018.8594106
18. Rau, A., et al.: Implicit domain adaptation with conditional generative adversarial networks for depth prediction in endoscopy. Int. J. Comput. Assist. Radiol. Surg. **14**(7), 1167–1176 (2019). https://doi.org/10.1007/s11548-019-01962-w
19. Ren, S., He, K., Girshick, R., Sun, J.: Faster r-cnn: towards real-time object detection with region proposal networks. Advances in Neural Information Processing Systems 28 (2015)
20. Ruijsink, B., et al.: Quality-aware semi-supervised learning for cmr segmentation. In: International Workshop on Statistical Atlases and Computational Models of the Heart, pp. 97–107. Springer (2020)
21. Scaradozzi, D., Zingaretti, S., Ferrari, A.: Simultaneous localization and mapping (slam) robotics techniques: a possible application in surgery. Shanghai Chest **2**(1) (2018). https://doi.org/10.21037/shc.2018.01.01
22. Sohn, K., et al.: Fixmatch: simplifying semi-supervised learning with consistency and confidence. Adv. Neural. Inf. Process. Syst. **33**, 596–608 (2020)
23. Sohn, K., Zhang, Z., Li, C.L., Zhang, H., Lee, C.Y., Pfister, T.: A simple semi-supervised learning framework for object detection. arXiv preprint arXiv:2005.04757 (2020)
24. van der Stap, N., van der Heijden, F., Broeders, I.A.M.J.: Towards automated visual flexible endoscope navigation. Surg. Endosc. **27**(10), 3539–3547 (2013). https://doi.org/10.1007/s00464-013-3003-7
25. Tarvainen, A., Valpola, H.: Mean teachers are better role models: Weight-averaged consistency targets improve semi-supervised deep learning results. Advances in Neural Information Processing Systems 30 (2017)
26. Xie, Q., Luong, M.T., Hovy, E., Le, Q.V.: Self-training with noisy student improves imagenet classification. In: Proceedings of the IEEE/CVF Conference on Computer Vision and Pattern Recognition, pp. 10687–10698 (2020)
27. Xu, M., et al.: End-to-end semi-supervised object detection with soft teacher. In: Proceedings of the IEEE/CVF International Conference on Computer Vision, pp. 3060–3069 (2021)
28. Yalniz, I.Z., Jégou, H., Chen, K., Paluri, M., Mahajan, D.: Billion-scale semi-supervised learning for image classification. arXiv preprint arXiv:1905.00546 (2019)
29. Yen, S.Y., et al.: Automatic lumen detection and magnetic alignment control for magnetic-assisted capsule colonoscope system optimization. Sci. Rep. **11**(1), 1–10 (2021). https://doi.org/10.1038/s41598-021-86101-9

SuperPoint Features in Endoscopy

O. León Barbed[1](✉), François Chadebecq[2], Javier Morlana[1],
José M. M. Montiel[1], and Ana C. Murillo[1]

[1] DIIS-i3A, University of Zaragoza, Zaragoza, Spain
`leon@unizar.es`
[2] WEISS, University College London, London, UK

Abstract. There is often a significant gap between research results and
applicability in routine medical practice. This work studies the performance of well-known local features on a medical dataset captured during
routine colonoscopy procedures. Local feature extraction and matching
is a key step for many computer vision applications, specially regarding 3D modelling. In the medical domain, handcrafted local features
such as SIFT, with public pipelines such as COLMAP, are still a pre-
dominant tool for this kind of tasks. We explore the potential of the
well known self-supervised approach SuperPoint [4], present an adapted
variation for the endoscopic domain and propose a challenging evaluation framework. SuperPoint based models achieve significantly higher
matching quality than commonly used local features in this domain. Our
adapted model avoids features within specularity regions, a frequent and
problematic artifact in endoscopic images, with consequent benefits for
matching and reconstruction results. Training code and models available
https://github.com/LeonBP/SuperPointEndoscopy.

Keywords: Deep learning · Self-supervision · Local features ·
Endoscopy

1   Introduction

Endoscopic procedures are a frequent medical practice. The endoscope guided
by the physician traverses hollow organs or body cavities, such as the colon.
Improvements in quality and efficiency of this kind of procedures can benefit
numerous patients and broaden screening campaigns reach. In endoscopy, as in
plenty other medical imaging tasks, computer vision has potential to help in
numerous aspects, such as assistance for diagnosis [33] or 3D modelling [13].
Unfortunately, there is still a significant gap between research results and applicability into the clinic, as discussed for example in [3]. This study emphasizes
the need for unsupervised methods that can fully exploit *in the wild* medical
data, which is in itself an already scarce resource. To move forward, it is often

Supplementary Information The online version contains supplementary material
available at https://doi.org/10.1007/978-3-031-21083-9_5.

L. Manfredi et al. (Eds.): ISGIE 2022/GRAIL 2022, LNCS 13754, pp. 45–55, 2022.
https://doi.org/10.1007/978-3-031-21083-9_5

SIFT   Ours   SIFT   Ours

Fig. 1. Feature extraction (red circle) and matching (green line) on endoscopy samples. (Color figure online)

key to consider challenging and realistic evaluations of current techniques, to determine where specific adaptations are needed.

Our work is motivated by the automated acquisition of 3D models of the endoluminal scene, that can facilitate augmented reality applications or assistance for navigation or patient monitoring. A core step in 3D reconstruction techniques, such as structure from motion (SfM) or Simultaneous Localization and Mapping (SLAM), is local feature detection and matching. Many broadly used SfM or SLAM frameworks still rely on hand-crafted local feature computation [17], although deep learning based techniques are boosting the state of the art. SuperPoint [4] is one of the seminal works in this topic and has inspired many follow up works discussed next. This promising research stream of learning based local features is recently being exploited in the endoscopic image domain [12], since evaluations and benchmarks on local feature detection and matching are typically focused on conventional images and mostly rigid scenes [10].

Endoscopic images captured during routine procedures present many challenges (such as challenging textures, frequent artifacts and scene deformation) that hinder local feature extraction. Figure 1 shows matches on two pairs of 1 second apart frames from a real colonoscopy where general purpose hand-crafted features (SIFT) can not tackle scenarios that our learned model features do. SIFT concentrates a lot on specularity artifacts, while our adapted SuperPoint model achieves more and better distributed matches, key for good 3D reconstructions. The main contributions of this work are: 1) A thorough study of SuperPoint effectiveness on *in the wild* endoscopic images, compared to typically used hand-crafted local features, including the proposed framework to evaluate these aspects in endoscopic data captured during daily medical practice; 2) our Superpoint adaptation to the endoscopic domain that improves its performance.

2   Related Work

Endoscopic Image Registration for 3D Reconstruction and Mapping in Minimally-Invasive Surgery. Endoscopic image registration is an open problem essential to image-guided intervention. Current efforts are directed at developing benchmarks and techniques able to tackle this challenging domain [2]. Learning-based approaches have shown their efficiency for general image registration, but they remain difficult to adapt to minimally-invasive imaging constraints, largely due to a lack of robust feature detection and matching in these scenarios.

Most vision-based approaches for 3D reconstruction in medical domains still rely on hand-crafted features [6,7]. Some works avoid the need for image registration by directly estimating and fusing key frames depth map [21] or combining them with camera pose estimates [16]. These pipelines get the input frames in a temporally consistent way. Our work is focused on a more general problem of feature extraction without any temporal information given to the model.

Local Feature Detection and Description for Image Registration. Image registration in general settings is a long studied problem [15]. A key aspect in this work is learning-based methods for image registration in endoscopy.

Early learning-based approaches solely focused on feature description. Advanced training loss and strategies significantly improved feature descriptor performances, e.g., by relying on triplet loss which aims at maximizing descriptor discrepancy between close but negative pairs of matches [18]. Similar results have been achieved by sampling more negative pairs as proposed in [29]. The learning-based feature detection problem has been less investigated. Former approaches learn to detect co-variant features and aim at reproducing and eventually improving hand-crafted feature detectors [5,11]. Unlike these approaches, [24] learns in an unsupervised way to rank keypoints according to their repeatability. The repeatability constraint is now generally combined with peakiness constraints for improving the robustness of the detector [19,32].

State-of-the-art registration approaches directly integrate feature extraction and description in a single framework. It has been shown that such approaches significantly improve matching results over classical hand-crafted feature-based registration methods [20]. Preliminary approaches such as LIFT [31] aim at reproducing the different stages of classical image registration pipelines. The need for Structure-from-Motion labels to train supervised methods makes these approaches impractical for applications such as endoscopy. More recent unsupervised approaches such as SuperPoint aim at jointly detecting and describing image landmarks [4]. The training is an iterative process that starts by learning from a synthetic dataset of random 2D shapes. The next iterations learn from the problem-specific dataset generated by applying random homographies to source images and using self-supervision from the previous iteration. It remains among the most efficient feature detection and description methods, and is still being considered in recent comparatives [10]. The R2D2 network [22], based on the L2-Quad architecture, jointly estimates a reliability and repeatability map together with a dense descriptor map. Despite their efficiency, methods jointly detecting and describing features are difficult to train and do not generalize well to different application domains [10]. To overcome these limitations, [30] propose to rely on a describe-to-detect strategy which takes advantage of the efficiency and performances of learning-based descriptor models. Recently, [14] propose a descriptor training strategy based on the formulation of a novel landmark tracking loss. While results demonstrate the efficacy of the proposed method, its computational cost remains generally high. Recent image matching trends propose dense matching as an intermediate step to local matching [34] and incorporating attention for the matching stages [9,23,28]. However, these approaches rely on 3D reconstruction ground truth for training, which is often not available for recordings acquired during routine medical practice.

3   SuperPoint in Endoscopy

Local feature matching is typically divided in four steps: feature detection, descriptor computation, matching and, often, outlier filtering. Our goal is to evaluate and improve existing methods on the first two steps for *in the wild* endoscopy imagery. The well-known SuperPoint, a seminal work regarding self-trained deep learning solutions for feature detection and description, is the base for our study. We next describe the Superpoint model variations used and the matching strategy applied. More implementation details in the supplementary material.

3.1   SuperPoint Models Considered

SuperPoint Base. Original SuperPoint model [4]. For this and the following model, we use the implementation by [8] , which allows us to use the original model weights as well as training new models. SuperPoint follows the known encoder-decoder architecture, but with two parallel decoders (detection and description heads). SuperPoint processes a single image ($I \in \mathbb{R}^{H \times W}$. H and W are the height and width, respectively) as input and produces two outputs: *detection*, image location of each keypoint extracted, and *description*, one descriptor for each keypoint. The *detection* head maps I into a tensor $\mathcal{X} \in \mathbb{R}^{H/8 \times W/8 \times 65}$. The depth of 65 corresponds to a cell of 8×8 pixels in I plus an additional channel called dustbin or "no interest point". After performing a softmax over the third dimension (we refer to it as softmd()), the dustbin is removed and the rest is reshaped to recover I's dimensions ($d2s(X) : \mathbb{R}^{H/8 \times W/8 \times 64} \rightarrow \mathbb{R}^{H \times W}$). The result is interpreted as a probability heatmap of the keypoints in the image. The *description* head maps I into a tensor $\mathcal{D} \in \mathbb{R}^{H/8 \times W/8 \times 256}$. The depth of 256 is the descriptor size, associated with a whole cell of 8×8 pixels in I. Bi-cubic interpolation is used to upsample $\mathcal{D}$ into having H and W as the first two dimensions. The descriptors are L2-normalized. SuperPoint is trained by contrasting the outputs of an image and a warped version of itself via a known homography and pre-computed pseudo-labels of image keypoints. The **loss function** is

$$\mathcal{L}_{SP}(\mathcal{X}, \mathcal{X}', \mathcal{D}, \mathcal{D}'; Y, Y', S) = \mathcal{L}_p(\mathcal{X}, Y) + \mathcal{L}_p(\mathcal{X}', Y') + \lambda \mathcal{L}_d(\mathcal{D}, \mathcal{D}', S), \quad (1)$$

where $\mathcal{X}$ and $\mathcal{X}'$ are the raw detection head outputs for image I and warped image I', respectively. Their associated detection pseudo-labels are Y and Y'. $\mathcal{D}$ and $\mathcal{D}'$ are the raw description head outputs. $S \in \mathbb{R}^{H/8 \times W/8 \times H/8 \times H/8}$ is the homography-induced correspondence matrix. $\mathcal{L}_p$ is the detection loss, which measures the discrepancies between the detection outputs and the pseudo-labels. $\mathcal{L}_d$ is the description loss, that forces descriptors that correspond to the same region in the original image to be similar, and different to the rest. λ is a weighting parameter.

E-SuperPoint. Specularities are very frequent artifacts in endoscopic images [27], and feature extractors often tend to detect features in the contour or within these image specularities. Features on specularities are not well suited for rigid model estimation, suffer from bad localization, and they turn out to be unreliable in downstream tasks such as tracking and 3D reconstruction. Although they can be masked out later, as we see in our experiments, they account for a too large portion of the features and matches. Thus, we aim to prevent them from happening in the first place, to encourage the detectors to focus on other regions.

We fine-tune the original model using endoscopic images (resized to 256 × 256) from routine medical practice recordings (dataset detailed in Sect. 4). Pseudo-labels are obtained with the original SuperPoint model. The pseudo-label is set to zero where the confidence value is lower than a threshold of 0.015. Non-maximum suppression is applied over windows of 9 × 9 pixels, and only the top 600 points are finally saved. We fine-tune the model for 200000 iterations with learning rate of 1e−5 and batch size of 2. We use sparse loss for more efficient convergence [8], and the rest of parameters are the same as they describe. For testing we set the detection threshold to 0.015 and non-maximum suppression over 3 × 3 windows.

Our modification of the SuperPoint model adds a new term to the training loss, our specularity loss $\mathcal{L}_s$. The purpose of $\mathcal{L}_s$ is to account for all the keypoints that are extracted on top of specularities, and is close to zero when there are no keypoints on those locations. **The final loss** is:

$$\mathcal{L}_{ESP}(I, I', \mathcal{X}, \mathcal{X}', \mathcal{D}, \mathcal{D}'; Y, Y', S) = \mathcal{L}_{SP}(\dots) + \lambda_s \mathcal{L}_s(\mathcal{X}, I) + \lambda_s \mathcal{L}_s(\mathcal{X}', I'), \quad (2)$$

where we add to the original $\mathcal{L}_{SP}$ the value of our specularity loss $\mathcal{L}_s$, once per image, weighted by the scale factor λ_s. $\mathcal{L}_s$ is defined as

$$\mathcal{L}_s(\mathcal{X}, I) = \frac{\sum_{h,w=1}^{H,W} [\mathrm{m}(I)_{hw} \cdot \mathrm{d2s}(\mathrm{softmd}(\mathcal{X}))_{hw}]}{\epsilon + \sum_{h,w=1}^{H,W} \mathrm{m}(I)_{hw}}, \quad (3)$$

where softmd() and d2s() are softmax and reshape functions from the original SuperPoint, and $\epsilon = 10^{-10}$. The subscript X_{hw} refers to the value of X at row h and column w. m(I) is a weighting mask: it is > 0 for pixels near a specularity and 0 otherwise. The mask comes from post-processing I with three operations: a binary threshold of $I_{hw} > 0.7$, a dilation of this binary output with a 3 × 3 kernel size, and a Gaussian blur of the mask with 9 × 9 kernel size and $\sigma = 4$. The threshold of 0.7 was chosen empirically, after observing that higher values missed too many specularities and lower values were discarding too many valid regions. To balance the new loss component $\mathcal{L}_s$, we set the weighting parameter $\lambda_s = 100$ so the losses have similar magnitudes for better optimization. Testing parameters remain the same.

3.2   SuperPoint Matching

SuperGlue [23] is a well-known matching strategy proposed for SuperPoint. However, it requires correspondence ground-truth for training so we can not easily adapt it to endoscopy imagery. We opt to use bi-directional brute force matching, the originally recommended matching for SuperPoint. We also perform a robust geometry estimation with RANSAC to remove outliers, assuming local rigidity for short periods of time. Matching of frames too far apart along the video would need to account for significant deformations, which is out of the scope for this work.

4   Experiments

This section summarizes the main results and insights from our comparison of different SuperPoint models and well-known local features applied in endoscopic data. Implementation details are in the supplementary material, Table 1.

Datasets. A key aspect in this research is to evaluate local feature performance on *in the wild* endoscopic recordings. The model is trained on a set of private videos, and evaluated on two public benchmarks: EndoMapper [1] and Hyper-Kvasir [2]. The supplementary material includes sample images from all sets.

- **Train set.** Endoscopy videos captured across several days of regular medical practice, each video corresponding to a routine procedure on a different patient. We use 11 videos and extract 125000 training frames and another 7179 for validation.
- **EndoMapper** *test set.* 6 full endoscopies for testing (14191 frames). Sequences 1, 2, 14, 16, 17 and 95. This dataset is similar to the videos used for training.
- **Hyper-Kvasir** *test set.* 31 short test videos (total of 51925 frames). The labeled videos in "lower-gi-tract/quality-of-mucosal-view/BBPS-2-3".

Evaluation Framework Proposed. As often discussed in recent literature, common matching quality metrics, such as repeatibility or homography estimation, are not fully representative of local features behaviour in real world settings [10]. This work also shows that hand-crafted features, particularly SIFT, can still surpass more recent deep learning based features regarding accuracy in 3D vision tasks such as image registration. For features and matches to be useful in posterior 3D reconstruction tasks, known desired properties include: good amount of quality matches (reliable and accurate) and matches covering all the scene to better capture the 3D scene information. We propose the following for the evaluation:

- To use an **existing SfM approach**, COLMAP [25,26], to **pre-compute a pseudo-ground truth** for the relative pose between each pair of frames. COLMAP runs a final global bundle adjustment optimization to recover all relative camera poses. This pseudo-ground truth is used to compute rotation estimation errors and matching quality metrics detailed next.
- A set of **matching quality metrics** to account for: 1) matching quantity and quality, with inliers obtained from Essential (when camera calibration is available, E Inl.) or Fundamental (F Inl.) matrix RANSAC-based estimation,

Table 1. Matching quality metrics for the two different test sets. E-SP trained on *Train set.* pGT only available for (a) EndoMapper data.

	Feat/Img	E Inl.	%*Gr*	pGT Inl.	%*Gr*	Feat/Img	F Inl.	%*Gr*
SIFT	2350.2	148.2	11.9	71.6	9.3	**825.7**	151.3	**18.6**
ORB	2163.0	153.0	8.5	80.9	6.0	361.3	137.2	6.3
SP Base	1333.7	96.4	11.4	57.1	8.2	211.8	51.3	11.1
E-SP	**4500.9**	**278.9**	**13.2**	**172.0**	**9.8**	591.3	**200.4**	11.3

(a) **EndoMapper** *test set* (1080x1080 resolution)   (b) **Hyper-Kvasir** (512x512)

and inliers according to the relative pose provided as pseudo-ground truth (pGT Inl.); 2) scene coverage, with image cell % (out of a 16×16 grid) with at least one inlier (*%Gr*).

Matching Quality Evaluation. The following experiments analyze how well each feature can be matched along challenging endoscopic sequences. We extract and match features across pairs of frames 1 second apart from each other from sequences in EndoMapper (1 second = 40 frames for three videos, 1 s = 50 frames for the other three) and Hyper-Kvasir (1 second = 25 frames).

Table 1 shows the performance of different baselines and our adapted model. The changes proposed have a noticeable effect, obtaining improvements in amount of features extracted and inlier matches (both with RANSAC and with the pseudo-GT) and spreading of these matches over the image in both scenarios. This is remarkable because E-SP was not fine-tuned in (b) Hyper-Kvasir data but it still mostly outperforms the rest.

Specularities. E-SuperPoint is designed to encourage feature extraction avoiding specularities. This experiment evaluates this with the number of features and inliers when features located in specularity pixels are discarded. We consider a pixel part of a specularity if the intensity value is over 0.7. Table 2 summarizes these results, showing that the baseline models lose a significant amount of features and inliers if we ignore specularity features (*w/o S*), confirming the suspicion that they fire too much on specularities in this environment. In contrast, the proposed E-SuperPoint effectively removes reliance in specularities and allows the detector to focus on other image patterns which have higher chances of being stable. Figure 2 shows several matching examples. Higher resolution version of them and additional examples can be found in the supplementary material.

Rotation Estimation from Matches. We compare the RANSAC-estimated essential matrix and the pseudo-ground truth essential matrix to compute the rotation estimation error for every pair of images. These values are summarized in Table 3, where we show the values of relevant percentiles of the errors obtained. E-SuperPoint achieves lower rotation error than all the other methods. Additionally, when counting the percentage of the estimations that obtain an error lower than 30 degrees, E-SuperPoint succeeds **71.6%** of the time, while the second best, SuperPoint Base, only 61.3%. Figure 2 shows some examples where we

Table 2. Influence of specularities in the matching results (in EndoMapper *test set*). all feat: total number; w/o S: number without features that fall into specularities.

	Feat/Img		E Inliers	
	All feat.	w/o S	All feat.	w/o S
SIFT	2350.2	2006.2 (85.4%)	148.2	129.1 (87.1%)
ORB	2163.0	867.7 (40.1%)	153.0	61.8 (40.4%)
SP Base	1333.7	1035.2 (77.6%)	96.4	73.5 (76.2%)
E-SP	4500.9	4431.3 (**98.5%**)	278.9	274.7 (98.5%)

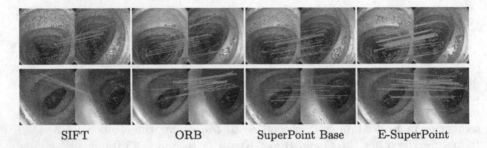

SIFT   ORB   SuperPoint Base   E-SuperPoint

Fig. 2. Features (red circles) and inlier matches after RANSAC (green lines) obtained for two pairs of 1 second apart frames using different features. (Color figure online)

Table 3. Rotation estimation error for pairs of frames 1 s apart. Percentile values of the errors obtained by each method.

Percentile	10th	20th	30th	40th	median
SIFT	3.2	5.5	8.4	12.4	20.1
ORB	3.7	7.3	13.4	27.4	45.8
SP Base	3.2	5.8	9.2	13.4	19.8
E-SP	**2.6**	**4.8**	**7.5**	**10.5**	**14.5**

can see that E-SuperPoint is more robust than other methods: Top row example shows how E-SuperPoint ignores the specularities in the image completely (there are no features extracted on top of it), and the bottom row example shows that our model finds more matches and better spread over the image than the other methods. The improvement is largely due to the adaptation we made to better deal with specularities for feature extraction.

5   Conclusions

This work[1] studies the performance of local features in *in the wild* endoscopic environments, using data captured during routine medical practice. We compare

[1] This project has been funded by the European Union's Horizon 2020 research and innovation programme under grant agreement No 863146 and Aragon Government FSE-T45_20R.

the effectiveness of hand-crafted local features against deep learning-based ones, in particular SIFT, ORB and SuperPoint. Although hand-crafted features are still a dominant choice in this field, we show how deep learning based features can surpass them in the considered challenging environments. Besides, we have trained and adapted the general-purpose SuperPoint to better fit the challenges of endoscopic imagery. Our evaluation, on endoscopies of different patients, is focused on the quality of the recovered 3D camera motion. Our results show that SuperPoint adaptation provides more numerous and non-specular features, and more disperse correspondences, essential for accurate and robust 3D geometry estimations.

References

1. Azagra, P., et al.: Endomapper dataset of complete calibrated endoscopy procedures. arXiv preprint arXiv:2204.14240 (2022)
2. Borgli, H., Thambawita, V., Smedsrud, P.H., Hicks, S., Jha, D., et al.: Hyperkvasir, a comprehensive multi-class image and video dataset for gastrointestinal endoscopy. Sci. Data **7**(1), 1–14 (2020)
3. Chadebecq, F., Vasconcelos, F., Mazomenos, E., Stoyanov, D.: Computer vision in the surgical operating room. Visceral Med. **36**(6), 456–462 (2020)
4. DeTone, D., Malisiewicz, T., Rabinovich, A.: Superpoint: self-supervised interest point detection and description. In: Conference on Computer Vision and Pattern Recognition Workshops. IEEE (2018)
5. Di Febbo, P., Dal Mutto, C., Tieu, K., Mattoccia, S.: KCNN: extremely-efficient hardware keypoint detection with a compact convolutional neural network. In: CVPR Workshops. IEEE (2018)
6. Espinel, Y., Calvet, L., Botros, K., Buc, E., Tilmant, C., Bartoli, A.: Using multiple images and contours for deformable 3D-2D registration of a preoperative CT in laparoscopic liver surgery. In: de Bruijne, M., et al. (eds.) MICCAI 2021. LNCS, vol. 12904, pp. 657–666. Springer, Cham (2021). https://doi.org/10.1007/978-3-030-87202-1_63
7. Gómez-Rodríguez, J.J., Lamarca, J., Morlana, J., Tardós, J.D., Montiel, J.M.: SD-DefSLAM: semi-direct monocular SLAM for deformable and intracorporeal scenes. In: International Conference on Robotics and Automation. IEEE (2021)
8. Jau, Y.Y., Zhu, R., Su, H., Chandraker, M.: Deep keypoint-based camera pose estimation with geometric constraints. In: International Conference on Intelligent Robots and Systems. IEEE (2020). https://github.com/eric-yyjau/pytorch-superpoint
9. Jiang, W., Trulls, E., Hosang, J., Tagliasacchi, A., Yi, K.M.: Cotr: correspondence transformer for matching across images. arXiv preprint arXiv:2103.14167 (2021)
10. Jin, Y., et al.: Image matching across wide baselines: from paper to practice. Int. J. Comput. Vis. **129**(2), 517–547 (2021)
11. Laguna, A.B., Riba, E., Ponsa, D., Mikolajczyk, K.: Key. Net: keypoint detection by handcrafted and learned CNN filters. In: ICCV. IEEE (2019)
12. Liao, C., Wang, C., Bai, J., Lan, L., Wu, X.: Deep learning for registration of region of interest in consecutive wireless capsule endoscopy frames. Comput. Meth. Programs Biomed. **208**, 106189 (2021)

13. Liu, X., et al: Reconstructing sinus anatomy from endoscopic video – towards a radiation-free approach for quantitative longitudinal assessment. In: Martel, A.L., et al. (eds.) MICCAI 2020. LNCS, vol. 12263, pp. 3–13. Springer, Cham (2020). https://doi.org/10.1007/978-3-030-59716-0_1
14. Liu, X., et al.: Extremely dense point correspondences using a learned feature descriptor. In: Conference on Computer Vision and Pattern Recognition. IEEE (2020)
15. Ma, J., Jiang, X., Fan, A., Jiang, J., Yan, J.: Image matching from handcrafted to deep features: a survey. Int. J. Comput. Vis. 1–57 (2020)
16. Ma, R., Wang, R., Pizer, S., Rosenman, J., McGill, S.K., Frahm, J.M.: Real-time 3D reconstruction of colonoscopic surfaces for determining missing regions. In: Shen, D., et al. (eds.) MICCAI 2019. LNCS, vol. 11768, pp. 573–582. Springer, Cham (2019). https://doi.org/10.1007/978-3-030-32254-0_64
17. Mahmoud, N., Collins, T., Hostettler, A., Soler, L., Doignon, C., Montiel, J.M.M.: Live tracking and dense reconstruction for handheld monocular endoscopy. IEEE Trans. Med. Imaging 38(1), 79–89 (2018)
18. Mishchuk, A., Mishkin, D., Radenović, F., Matas, J.: Working hard to know your neighbor's margins: local descriptor learning loss. In: International Conference on Neural Information Processing Systems (2017)
19. Mishkin, D., Radenovic, F., Matas, J.: Repeatability is not enough: learning affine regions via discriminability. In: ECCV (2018)
20. Ono, Y., Trulls, E., Fua, P., Yi, K.M.: LF-Net: learning local features from images. In: International Conference on Neural Information Processing Systems (2018)
21. Ozyoruk, K.B., et al.: EndoSLAM dataset and an unsupervised monocular visual odometry and depth estimation approach for endoscopic videos. Med. Image Anal. 71, 102058 (2021)
22. Revaud, J., Weinzaepfel, P., de Souza, C.R., Humenberger, M.: R2D2: repeatable and reliable detector and descriptor. In: International Conference on Neural Information Processing Systems (2019)
23. Sarlin, P.E., DeTone, D., Malisiewicz, T., Rabinovich, A.: Superglue: learning feature matching with graph neural networks. In: Conference on Computer Vision and Pattern Recognition. IEEE (2020)
24. Savinov, N., Seki, A., Ladický, L., Sattler, T., Pollefeys, M.: Quad-networks: unsupervised learning to rank for interest point detection. In: Conference on Computer Vision and Pattern Recognition. IEEE (2017)
25. Schönberger, J.L., Frahm, J.M.: Structure-from-motion revisited. In: CVPR. IEEE (2016)
26. Schönberger, J.L., Zheng, E., Pollefeys, M., Frahm, J.M.: Pixelwise view selection for unstructured multi-view stereo. In: European Conference on Computer Vision (2016)
27. Stoyanov, D., Yang, G.Z.: Removing specular reflection components for robotic assisted laparoscopic surgery. In: International Conference on Image Processing. IEEE (2005)
28. Sun, J., Shen, Z., Wang, Y., Bao, H., Zhou, X.: Loftr: detector-free local feature matching with transformers. In: CVPR. IEEE (2021)
29. Tian, Y., Fan, B., Wu, F.: L2-Net: deep learning of discriminative patch descriptor in euclidean space. In: Conference on Computer Vision and Pattern Recognition. IEEE (2017)
30. Tian, Y., Balntas, V., Ng, T., Barroso-Laguna, A., Demiris, Y., Mikolajczyk, K.: D2d: keypoint extraction with describe to detect approach. In: ACCV (2020)

31. Yi, K.M., Trulls, E., Lepetit, V., Fua, P.: LIFT: learned Invariant Feature Transform. In: Leibe, B., Matas, J., Sebe, N., Welling, M. (eds.) ECCV 2016. LNCS, vol. 9910, pp. 467–483. Springer, Cham (2016). https://doi.org/10.1007/978-3-319-46466-4_28
32. Zhang, L., Rusinkiewicz, S.: Learning to detect features in texture images. In: Conference on Computer Vision and Pattern Recognition. IEEE (2018)
33. Zhang, Z., Xie, Y., Xing, F., McGough, M., Yang, L.: Mdnet: a semantically and visually interpretable medical image diagnosis network. In: CVPR. IEEE (2017)
34. Zhou, Q., Sattler, T., Leal-Taixe, L.: Patch2pix: epipolar-guided pixel-level correspondences. In: CVPR. IEEE (2021)

Estimating the Coverage in 3D Reconstructions of the Colon from Colonoscopy Videos

Emmanuelle Muhlethaler$^{(\boxtimes)}$, Erez Posner, and Moshe Bouhnik

Intuitive Surgical, Inc., Sunnyvale, CA, USA
{emmanuelle.muhlethaler,erez.posner,moshe.bouhnik}@intusurg.com

Abstract. Colonoscopy is the most common procedure for early detection and removal of polyps, a critical component of colorectal cancer prevention. Insufficient visual coverage of the colon surface during the procedure often results in missed polyps. To mitigate this issue, reconstructing the 3D surfaces of the colon in order to visualize the missing regions has been proposed. However, robustly estimating the local and global coverage from such a reconstruction has not been thoroughly investigated until now. In this work, we present a new method to estimate the coverage from a reconstructed colon pointcloud. Our method splits a reconstructed colon into segments and estimates the coverage of each segment by estimating the area of the missing surfaces. We achieve a mean absolute coverage error of 3–6% on colon segments generated from synthetic colonoscopy data and real colonography CT scans. In addition, we show good qualitative results on colon segments reconstructed from real colonoscopy videos.

1 Introduction

Colorectal cancer is the third most common cancer worldwide [1]. The early detection and removal of polyps during routine colonoscopy is an essential component of colorectal cancer prevention. The procedure is based on a visual examination of the colon using a single camera mounted on a flexible tube. During this procedure, 22%-28% of polyps are missed [12,18], often because they never appeared in the field of view of the camera [12].

In recent years, efforts were made [8,16,17,25] to estimate the colonoscopy *coverage*, that is, the fraction of the colon surface examined during a colonoscopy procedure. We define the coverage as the ratio: $\frac{S_{examined}}{S_{total}}$ where $S_{examined}$ is the area of the surface examined during the procedure and S_{total} the area of the entire visible surface, including the missed regions. One possible approach to the coverage estimation problem is to compute a 3D reconstruction of the colon from the colonoscopy video [16,17,25]. The missed regions will appear as holes in the

---

Supplementary Information The online version contains supplementary material available at https://doi.org/10.1007/978-3-031-21083-9_6.

reconstructed mesh. In this paper, we focus on the computation of the coverage given a 3d reconstruction of the colon. This has only briefly been addressed until now, as most works tend to focus on the 3d reconstruction itself.

We assume a reconstruction of the colon with holes and devise a method to estimate the coverage *per segment*, where a segment is defined based on the colon centerline. Estimating the coverage per segment provides a more detailed and useful information than a global colon coverage estimation. For instance, if the coverage estimation is run during a colonoscopy procedure, an estimation of the coverage per segment, rather than for the whole procedure, can allow the physician to easily identify the regions where the coverage is deficient and revisit the uninspected areas. We choose to base our method on the 3d completion of the reconstructed colon surface, thus providing an estimation of the location and shape of the missing surfaces, in addition to their area. Such an approach hasn't been explored yet, and makes our method easily interpretable, allowing us to visually assess the reliability of our coverage estimation when ground truth is unavailable. The central component of our method is a *per segment coverage and centerline estimation module*, composed of 3 parts (see Fig. 1):

1. A **point completion network**, inspired by 3D-EPN [5]. It takes as input a heatmap representing a partial colon segment (i.e with holes) and outputs a heatmap of the completed segment together with its centerline.
2. A **centerline extraction algorithm**, to extract the centerline from the estimated heatmap.
3. A **mesh extraction algorithm**, to extract the surface mesh from the estimated heatmap.

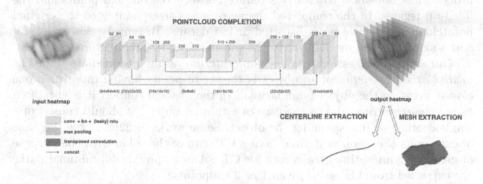

Fig. 1. The coverage estimation per segment, composed of three parts: Pointcloud completion, centerline extraction, mesh extraction.

2   Related Works

A number of works address the problem of constructing a 3d model of the colon from colonoscopy videos. In [11], the colon surface is generated based on folds detection and a depth from intensity model, but is limited to the reconstruction of single-frame segments. More recently, Ma et al. [16] used a SLAM backbone based on DSO [7] together with a recurrent neural network for pose and depth estimation, to successfully reconstruct colon surfaces from real colonoscopy videos. They estimate the coverage on 12 real data segments, by mapping the surfaces onto a 2D rectangular frame, but no ground truth is available to measure the accuracy of the method. Zhang et al. [25] use a non rigid registration between a mesh model from a prior CT colonoscopy and a 3D reconstruction based on deep depth estimation and classic sparse features. This method is not applicable to most real life scenarios, where no CT scan is available. Posner et al. [17] use deep depth estimation and deep features to reconstruct 3D surfaces from colonoscopy videos. In contrast to other works, Freedman et al. [8] chose to avoid building a 3D reconstruction and instead train a number of networks to directly estimate the coverage from a sequence of images. This method provides an estimate of the coverage per segment, but has a few drawbacks, such as lack of interpretability and the fact that a segment is defined based on time (a fixed number of frames), and does not represent a physical colon segment of a given length.

We choose to base our method on the 3d completion of reconstructed colon pointclouds. The task of estimating complete 3D shapes from partial observations has many applications in computer vision and robotics. Recent solutions to the pointcloud completion problem can be roughly classified according to the type of deep architecture used. The earlier works are CNN based, and represent the pointcloud as a voxel grid [5,10,20]. An important limitation of this approach is the loss of resolution caused by the voxelization of the shape. Another approach consists of using a PointNet [4] type of architecture [21,24], where a decoder reconstructs the complete pointcloud from a global learned feature. This process does not allow to clearly separate between the original points and the filled-up regions. In the completed shape, regions corresponding to the original pointcloud might have been distorted or lost details. To remedy this issue, [23] add a skip attention mechanism to the encoder decoder architecture.

Our method also estimates the colon *centerline*, as an intermediate step. The *medial axis* or *skeleton* of an object is the set of points having more than one closest point on the object boundary [3]. In the medical context it is also often called the *centerline*, and in the case of a tubular object, it should consist of a single continuous line spanning the object. Some works [6,22] address the issue of extracting the colon centerline from a CT scan of the colon with the purpose of generating an optimal trajectory for CT colonography. In [6] minimal paths are extracted from CT scans given 1 or 2 endpoints.

3   Coverage Estimation of 3D Colon Reconstructions

Our method estimates the coverage per segment of a 3D pointcloud representing a colon with holes. For maximum generality, we assume that our input consists only of a set of points $P = \{p_i\}$, $p_i \in \mathbb{R}^3$ with no further information.

We define a *segment* using the centerline. The centerline is split into a number of continuous segments of a given arc length (e.g. $l = 7$ cm). For each centerline segment, the corresponding colon segment is defined by two cross sections perpendicular to the centerline (see Fig. 2).

3.1 Dataset

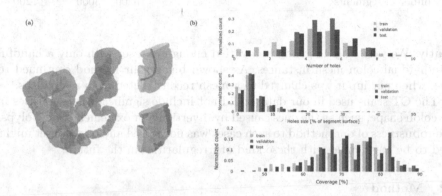

Fig. 2. (a) Colon from our CT scan dataset, together with a magnified cropped segment and its corresponding centerline and generated holes. (b) Distribution of holes number, sizes and coverage in our dataset. The individual holes sizes are expressed as a percentage of the segment surface.

Our training dataset is made of both CT and synthetic data. For the CT data, we used 3 colon meshes manually segmented from a dataset of colonography CT scans [19]. As the resulting pointclouds do not contain any holes, we generated holes ourselves, by randomly cropping out spheres of various radii (see Fig. 2 (a)). The generated distributions of coverage, holes numbers and holes sizes are displayed on the figure Fig. 2. The synthetic data consists of synthetic colonoscopy videos from which a reconstructed mesh can be generated. The various holes permutations were generated using a synthetic camera with random poses inside the colon. Using these meshes, we generated a dataset of colon segments to train and test our coverage estimation module. See Table 1. For each segment in our train and validation set, 15 permutations corresponding to a different set of holes were generated. Each segment in our dataset also has a corresponding centerline. The centerlines were calculated on the full colon meshes using a classic skeleton extraction algorithm, in which the parameters were manually tuned for each mesh and the result was refined to obtain the desired properties (connectivity, centricity and singularity). These centerlines were used to split the original colons into segments (arc length $l \in [5, 6, 7]$) and to provide a GT centerline for our network training.

While the overall shape of a colon varies enormously between people, we found that reducing our problem to segments (with scale, rotation, deformation and noise augmentations added during training) allowed for the training on one colon to generalize well to another, even when the overall shape differed

Table 1. Dataset summary. A, B represent the colons of our synthetic dataset and a, b, c the colons of our CT dataset.

	Train	Validation	Test
Colon meshes [a, b, c] ∈ CT scans; [A, B] ∈ synthetic	a, b, A	a, b, A	c, B
Number of segments	10200	3000	1200

greatly. We were able to generate a varied enough dataset with only a handful of individual colon mesh instances. As shown below, our method continued to work when our input was changed to a mesh reconstructed from real videos.

The CT scans used in our dataset did not include significant irregularities in the colon shape, such as the ones caused by diverticula or extremely large polyps. The robustness of our method to such cases was not tested and our dataset might need to be augmented with these kind of irregularities in the future.

3.2   Method

Pointcloud Completion. Similarly to 3D-EPN [5], we used a 3DCNN to complete a pointcloud represented by voxel grid. Although this type of approach suffers from a loss of resolution due to the voxelization of the shape, it is mitigated in our case by the following: (1) the full colon can consistently be split into small enough segments to get a satisfying resolution, (2) our main goal being coverage estimation, a loss of resolution is acceptable as long as it does not affect the coverage. We replaced the 3D-EPN architecture by 3dUNet [26], having observed that the fully connected layer of 3D-EPN [5] degraded the performance of our network. It might be related to the fact that, in contrast to classic shape completion networks, no object class needed to be encoded here. Our dataset consists of a single class of objects with a strongly constrained geometry.

We defined a customized input and target representation for our problem, which is both easy to learn and from which a mesh and centerline with desired properties can be easily extracted. Our input is a 3D heatmap representing the partial colon segment (i.e. with holes). Our target is a 3D heatmap representing the centerline and completed segment. The heatmaps $\mathbf{H}_{input}$, $\mathbf{H}_{target}$, are $64 \times 64 \times 64$ voxel grids and are defined in the following way, for a voxel $\mathbf{v}$:

$$\mathbf{H}_{input}[\mathbf{v}] = \tanh(0.2 * d(\mathbf{v}, \mathbf{S_0}))$$

$$\mathbf{H}_{target}[\mathbf{v}] = \frac{\tanh(0.2 * d(\mathbf{v}, \mathbf{S_1}))}{\tanh(0.2 * d(\mathbf{v}, \mathbf{S_1})) + \tanh(0.2 * d(\mathbf{v}, \mathbf{C}))}$$

where $d(\mathbf{v}, \mathbf{S_0})$ is the euclidean distance between $\mathbf{v}$ and the voxelized partial segment $\mathbf{S_0}$, $d(\mathbf{v}, \mathbf{S_1})$ is the euclidean distance between $\mathbf{v}$ and the voxelized complete segment $\mathbf{S_1}$, and $d(\mathbf{v}, \mathbf{C})$ is the euclidean distance between $\mathbf{v}$ and the voxelized centerline $\mathbf{C}$. The input heatmap is zero at the position of the (partial) segment surface and increases rapidly towards 1 away from it. The target heatmap is zero at the position of the (complete) segment surface, increases towards 1 at the position of the centerline, and converges to 0.5 everywhere else. Both heatmaps are illustrated in Fig. 1. We use an L2 loss to train the network.

Centerline Extraction. The centerline is a key component of our pipeline. It allows us to split the colon into well defined segments and is also used for mesh extraction. Our output heatmap contains high values at the center of the colon, but simply thresholding the heatmap does not yield a singular and connected path. We use instead a minimal path extraction technique, similar to [6]. We add to it an initial step to calculate the start and end points of the centerline, which we don't know in general. To estimate the centerline start and end points, we create a nearest neighbor graph from the voxels with values $> 1 - \delta$ in our heatmap (which roughly correlates to the centerline). The shortest path between all pairs is calculated and the longest path among them is selected. We use the extremities of this path as our centerline start and end points. We then compute the travel time from the starting point to each voxel in the volume, using the fast marching algorithm [2] and our heatmap as speed map. The centerline is extracted by backpropagating the travel time from the end point down to the starting point. The different steps of our method are illustrated in Fig. 3.

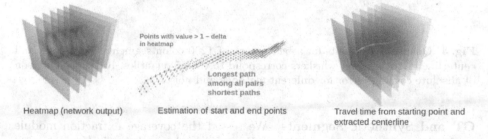

Heatmap (network output)   Estimation of start and end points   Travel time from starting point and extracted centerline

Points with value > 1 – delta in heatmap

Longest path among all pairs shortest paths

Fig. 3. Centerline extraction steps

Coverage Estimation. Our estimation of the coverage includes 3 main steps: (1) Extract the completed pointcloud or mesh from the voxel grid, (2) differentiate between the filled up regions (the holes) and the rest of the pointcloud, (3) Calculate the ratio of the partial surface to the complete surface.

The completed surface could be extracted by thresholding the predicted heatmap and extracting voxels with values close to 0. We found that with such a method, the extracted pointcloud can vary in thickness, making the calculation of the coverage (step 3) difficult. We opt instead to extract the completed mesh using marching cubes [14] in a neighborhood of the zeros-valued pixels. The surface to extract corresponds to a heatmap minima rather than an isovalue (with larger values on one side of the surface and smaller values on the other). We solve this issue by replacing the value of each voxel $\mathbf{v}$ in the neighborhood of the surface by $\mathbf{v}_{new} = d(\mathbf{s}, \mathbf{C}) - d(\mathbf{v}, \mathbf{C})$, where $\mathbf{s}$ is the surface voxel closest to

$\mathbf{v}$, $d(\mathbf{s}, \mathbf{C})$ is euclidean distance between $\mathbf{s}$ and the centerline, and $d(\mathbf{v}, \mathbf{C})$ is the euclidean distance between the $\mathbf{v}$ and the centerline. Once the completed mesh is extracted, holes are identified by comparison to the original partial pointcloud. We classify as belonging to a hole any vertex in the completed mesh with a distance to the partial pointcloud larger than $\sqrt{3}$ voxel size. The coverage is computed by dividing the partial mesh surface by the complete mesh surface.

This per segment coverage estimation module can then be integrated into a broader pipeline, where the reconstructed colon is split into segments and the coverage is estimated per segment.

4   Results

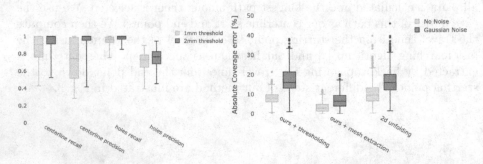

Fig. 4. Quantitative results on a benchmark of 1200 colon segments. Left: holes and centerline metrics. Lower whiskers correspond to the q5 quantiles. Right: Comparison of absolute coverage error for different methods and noises.

CT and Synthetic Segments. We tested the coverage extraction module on 1200 segments from our test set. We used both regular noiseless data and segments to which gaussian noise ($\sigma = 0.5$ mm) was added. We compared: (1) our coverage estimation method with the mesh extraction replaced by thresholding, (2) our full coverage estimation method and (3) the 2D unwrapping method described in [16]. In [16], a straight line was used as centerline, which is not possible in general on curved segments. We chose to use our learned centerline instead. As shown on Fig. 4, we obtain the lowest absolute coverage error (3% and 6% MAE respectively on noiseless and noise augmented data) when using our learned heatmap together with mesh extraction. We observed that all methods tended to be biased towards underestimating the coverage, i.e. overestimating the surface of the holes. In the case of ours + mesh extraction method, it seems that the main reason for this bias is the detection of nonexistent holes at the extremities of the segment (see Fig. 5). These errors are usually removed when we have access to the surface of adjacent segments.

We evaluate our centerline and holes estimation using the metrics: precision = $\text{mean}_{\mathbf{p}_{est}}(\min_{\mathbf{p}_{gt}} \|\mathbf{p}_{est} - \mathbf{p}_{gt}\| < th)$, recall = $\text{mean}_{\mathbf{p}_{gt}}(\min_{\mathbf{p}_{est}} \|\mathbf{p}_{est} - \mathbf{p}_{gt}\| < th)$, where $th \in [1\text{min}, 2\text{mm}]$ and $\mathbf{p}_{gt}$, $\mathbf{p}_{est}$ are respectively GT and estimated 3d points. The choice of thresholds is both related to the resolution of our heatmap (around 1mm for a 6cm segment voxelized into a $64 \times 64 \times 64$ voxel grid) and to the fact that 1mm corresponds to the lowest range of polyp sizes [13]. We achieve very high precision and recall, in particular for the centerline, with a median value of 1.0 for both precision and recall. We observed that most of our outliers could be traced back to a wrong estimation of the centerline extremities. Training our network with a stronger emphasis on the centerline might mitigate this issue.

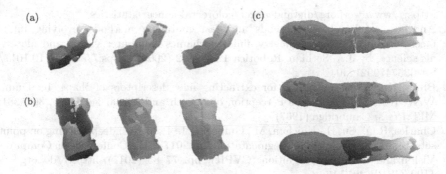

Fig. 5. Holes and centerline estimation on (a) CT scans segments, (b) 3d rigid colon print reconstruction, (c) colon 10K reconstruction. Each triplet represents: the input segment, the completed mesh with holes in red, the completed mesh with centerline in red. Additional examples are available in the supplementary material

Rigid Colon Print and Real Data. We additionally tested our method on surfaces reconstructed from (1) a video recorded using a colonoscope of a colon 3d rigid print [17], (2) a real optical colonoscopy video from the Colon10K dataset [15]. In both cases, the reconstruction was obtained using the method described in [17]. We obtained good qualitative results (see Fig. 5). The segments obtained by running the reconstruction [17] on the real colonoscopy sequences [15] didn't exhibit any holes. This is due to both the data and the reconstruction algorithm. On the data side, the colon segments of [15] tended to be particularly smooth, with very small haustral folds. On the reconstruction side, the deep monocular depth estimation tended to smooth out discontinuities, a known phenomena [9]. To obtain reconstructions with enough holes to test our method, we used 3 different subsets of the original frame sequences. We generated this way 3 sets of mesh with holes. Using the complete sequence reconstruction as ground truth for the full mesh (without holes), we obtained the following absolute coverage errors of: 5.2%, 3.8% and 7.6%. We found our method slightly more prone to errors when applied to this data, especially in cases where the reconstruction is noisy or contains errors. Training our network using more realistic noise augmentations and/or some actual reconstruction data (e.g. reconstruction from synthetic data colonoscopy) might help making our method more robust to these kind of failures.

5   Conclusion

We presented a novel method for estimating coverage given a 3d reconstruction of a colonoscopy procedure. Our method can be used to provide robust and interpretable local coverage feedback during a colonoscopy procedure, with 3D visualization of the missed surfaces.

References

1. https://www.wcrf.org/dietandcancer/colorectal-cancer-statistics/
2. Andrew, A.: Level set methods and fast marching methods: evolving interfaces in computational geometry, fluid mechanics, computer vision, and materials science, by J.A. Sethian. Robotica **18**, 89–92 (2000). https://doi.org/10.1017/S0263574799212404
3. Blum, H.: A transformation for extracting new descriptors of shape. In: Dunn, W.W. (ed.) Models for the Perception of Speech and Visual Form, pp. 362–381. MIT Press, Cambridge (1967)
4. Charles, R.Q., Su, H., Kaichun, M., Guibas, L.J.: PointNet: deep learning on point sets for 3D classification and segmentation. In: 2017 IEEE Conference on Computer Vision and Pattern Recognition (CVPR), pp. 77–85 (2017). https://doi.org/10.1109/CVPR.2017.16
5. Dai, A., Qi, C.R., Nießner, M.: Shape completion using 3D-encoder-predictor CNNs and shape synthesis. In: Proceedings of the Computer Vision and Pattern Recognition (CVPR). IEEE (2017)
6. Deschamps, T., Cohen, L.D.: Minimal paths in 3D images and application to virtual endoscopy. In: Vernon, D. (ed.) ECCV 2000. LNCS, vol. 1843, pp. 543–557. Springer, Heidelberg (2000). https://doi.org/10.1007/3-540-45053-X_35
7. Engel, J., Koltun, V., Cremers, D.: Direct sparse odometry. arXiv:1607.02565, July 2016
8. Freedman, D., et al.: Detecting deficient coverage in colonoscopies (2020)
9. Godard, C., Aodha, O.M., Brostow, G.J.: Digging into self-supervised monocular depth estimation. CoRR abs/1806.01260 (2018). http://arxiv.org/abs/1806.01260
10. Han, X., Li, Z., Haibin, H., Kalogerakis, E., Yu, Y.: High-resolution shape completion using deep neural networks for global structure and local geometry inference, October 2017. https://doi.org/10.1109/ICCV.2017.19
11. Hong, D., Tavanapong, W., Wong, J., Oh, J., Groen, P.: 3D reconstruction of virtual colon structures from colonoscopy images. Comput. Med. Imaging Graph. Off. J. Comput. Med. Imaging Soc. **38** (2013). https://doi.org/10.1016/j.compmedimag.2013.10.005
12. Leufkens, A., Van Oijen, M., Vleggaar, F., Siersema, P.: Factors influencing the miss rate of polyps in a back-to-back colonoscopy study. Endoscopy **44**(05), 470–475 (2012)
13. Lieberman, D., Moravec, M., Holub, J., Michaels, L., Eisen, G.: Polyp size and advanced histology in patients undergoing colonoscopy screening: implications for CT colonography. Gastroenterology **135**, 1100–5 (2008). https://doi.org/10.1053/j.gastro.2008.06.083
14. Lorensen, W.E., Cline, H.E.: Marching cubes: a high resolution 3D surface construction algorithm. In: Stone, M.C. (ed.) SIGGRAPH, pp. 163–169. ACM (1987). http://dblp.uni-trier.de/db/conf/siggraph/siggraph1987.html#LorensenC87

15. Ma, R., et al.: Colon10k: a benchmark for place recognition in colonoscopy. In: 2021 IEEE 18th International Symposium on Biomedical Imaging (ISBI), pp. 1279–1283 (2021). https://doi.org/10.1109/ISBI48211.2021.9433780
16. Ma, R., et al.: RNNSLAM: reconstructing the 3D colon to visualize missing regions during a colonoscopy. Med. Image Anal. **72**, 102100 (2021). https://doi.org/10.1016/j.media.2021.102100
17. Posner, E., Zholkover, A., Frank, N., Bouhnik, M.: C^3fusion: consistent contrastive colon fusion, towards deep slam in colonoscopy (2022). https://doi.org/10.48550/ARXIV.2206.01961. https://arxiv.org/abs/2206.01961
18. van Rijn, J.C., Reitsma, J.B., Stoker, J., Bossuyt, P.M., van Deventer, S.J., Dekker, E.: Polyp miss rate determined by tandem colonoscopy: a systematic review. Am. J. Gastroenterol. **101**(2), 343—350 (2006). https://doi.org/10.1111/j.1572-0241.2006.00390.x
19. Smith, K., et al.: Data from CT colonography. The cancer imaging archive (2015). https://doi.org/10.7937/K9/TCIA.2015.NWTESAY1
20. Stutz, D., Geiger, A.: Learning 3D shape completion from laser scan data with weak supervision. In: Proceedings of the IEEE Conference on Computer Vision and Pattern Recognition (CVPR), June 2018
21. Tchapmi, L.P., Kosaraju, V., Rezatofighi, H., Reid, I., Savarese, S.: TopNet: structural point cloud decoder. In: 2019 IEEE/CVF Conference on Computer Vision and Pattern Recognition (CVPR), pp. 383–392 (2019). https://doi.org/10.1109/CVPR.2019.00047
22. Wan, M., Liang, Z., Ke, Q., Hong, L., Bitter, I., Kaufman, A.: Automatic centerline extraction for virtual colonoscopy. IEEE Trans. Med. Imaging **21**(12), 1450–1460 (2002). https://doi.org/10.1109/TMI.2002.806409
23. Wen, X., Li, T., Han, Z., Liu, Y.S.: Point cloud completion by skip-attention network with hierarchical folding. In: 2020 IEEE/CVF Conference on Computer Vision and Pattern Recognition (CVPR), pp. 1936–1945 (2020). https://doi.org/10.1109/CVPR42600.2020.00201
24. Yuan, W., Khot, T., Held, D., Mertz, C., Hebert, M.: PCN: point completion network. In: 2018 International Conference on 3D Vision (3DV), pp. 728–737 (2018)
25. Zhang, S., Zhao, L., Huang, S., Ma, R., Hu, B., Hao, Q.: 3D reconstruction of deformable colon structures based on preoperative model and deep neural network. In: 2021 IEEE International Conference on Robotics and Automation (ICRA), pp. 1875–1881 (2021). https://doi.org/10.1109/ICRA48506.2021.9561772
26. Çiçek, Ö., Abdulkadir, A., Lienkamp, S.S., Brox, T., Ronneberger, O.: 3D U-Net: learning dense volumetric segmentation from sparse annotation (2016)

Graphs in Biomedical Image Analysis

Modular Graph Encoding and Hierarchical Readout for Functional Brain Network Based eMCI Diagnosis

Lang Mei[1,2,3], Mianxin Liu[1], Lingbin Bian[1], Yuyao Zhang[2], Feng Shi[3], Han Zhang[1], and Dinggang Shen[1,3(✉)]

[1] School of Biomedical Engineering, Shanghaitech University, Shanghai, China
dgshen@shanghaitech.edu.cn
[2] School of Information Science and Technology, Shanghaitech University, Shanghai, China
[3] Shanghai United Imaging Intelligence Co., Ltd., Shanghai, China

Abstract. The functional brain network, estimated from functional magnetic resonance imaging (fMRI), have been widely used to capture subtle brain function abnormality and perform diagnosis of brain diseases, such as early mild cognitive impairment (eMCI), i.e., with Graph Convolutional Network (GCN). However, there are at least two issues with GCN-based diagnosis methods, i.e., (1) over-smoothed representation of nodal features after using general convolutional kernels, and (2) simple blind readout of graph features without considering hierarchical organizations of brain functions. To address these two issues, we propose a GCN-based architecture (HFBN-GCN), based on the hierarchical functional brain network (defined with priors from brain atlases). Specifically, first, we design a "topology-focused brain encoder" to enhance nodal features by using (1) one branch of GCNs to focus on limited message passing among functional modules of each hierarchical level for alleviating over-smoothing issue and (2) another branch of GCNs to processes whole brain network for retaining original communication of information. Second, we design a "hierarchical brain readout" to utilize pre-defined hierarchical information to guide the coarse-to-fine readout process. We evaluate our proposed HFBN-GCN on the ADNI dataset with 910 fMRI data. Our proposed method achieves 73.4% accuracy (with 77.1% sensitivity and 71.1% specificity) in eMCI diagnosis, where both proposed strategies help boost performance compared to simply-stacked GCNs. In addition, our method suggests the dorsal attention network, saliency network and default mode network as the most crucial functional sub-networks for eMCI identifications. Our method thus is potentially beneficial for both clinical applications and neurological studies.

Keywords: fMRI · Graph convolutional network · Early mild cognitive impairment

L. Manfredi et al. (Eds.): ISGIE 2022/GRAIL 2022, LNCS 13754, pp. 69–78, 2022.
https://doi.org/10.1007/978-3-031-21083-9_7

1 Introduction

Mild cognitive impairment (MCI) manifests as a prodromal status of various types of dementia, induced by such as Alzheimer's disease (AD). During the MCI state, timely diagnoses and interventions can slow down or even reverse the progression to the serious cognitive inability. However, in an even earlier stage, i.e., early-stage MCI (eMCI), conventional methods based on behavior assessment and brain anatomical alternation are not sensitive enough to capture the subtle brain abnormality [10].

Recent studies suggest that the altered brain dynamics revealed by fMRI hold great potential for eMCI identification [7,19]. The fMRI-based brain studies have been growing increasingly in the last decades [12], where the functional connectivity (FC) is a representative measurement calculated from blood-oxygen-level-dependent (BOLD) signals. He FC characterizes the strength of information exchange between brain regions of interest (ROIs) as the level of temporal synchronization, which can typically be quantified as the correlation of BOLD signals between ROIs with the entire time series [21]. The functional brain network is a graph representation of the brain organization, where ROIs are defined as nodes and the FCs as edges. In the literature, the conventional methods use the graph-theory based metrics to extract and select distinguishing features to identify eMCIs [1,5]. More recently, studies based on deep learning increasingly tend to use graph neural networks (GNNs), which shows great power in processing non-Euclidean spatial data [18]. Despite the advancement compared to those traditional methods, two issues of the current GNN-based diagnostic methods remain unsolved.

First, the classical GNNs, such as graph convolutional network (GCN), suffer globally over-smoothed graph encoding after several layers of processing, resulting in homogeneous encoded features across nodes (region of interest, ROIs) [9,13]. This issue roots deeply in GCN's unlimited message passing within the graph, which diminishes the uniqueness of some important nodes in brain network [15]. Recent development has been made by the graph attention network (GAT) [16] and frequency adaptation graph convolutional networks (FAGCN) [3], both attempting to learn an extra weight between nodes to alleviate the over-smoothing problem. But these data-driven methods can still sensitive to noise and could identify so-called important nodes not aligning to the neuroscience prior. Second, after the encoding, when generating diagnosis results based on the encoded features via a readout process, many studies blindly pool the features using global averaging or the global maximum [22]. This again diminishes rich brain structure information, such as functional modules, which are shown to be crucial for brain information processing and thus should be considered under detecting brain disorders [2].

The latest advance from neuroscience provides a set of atlases to characterize the hierarchy of brain [14,20], which provides a layered and structured mapping from small brain regions to large brain sub-systems. Based on this prior knowledge, in this paper, we propose a GCN-based architecture guided by hierarchical functional brain network (HFBN-GCN), aiming to simultaneously address the over-smoothing and the blind readout problems, by incorporating the prior of the brain network hierarchy into GCN framework. Specifically, the novelty of our method includes two aspects: (1) A topology-focused GCN-based encoder to retain the particularity of regions. Asides from a series of stocked GCNs working on the whole network, another branch of GCNs is introduced to process limited sub-graphs defined at different scales of the brain hierarchy; (2) A hierarchical pooling module, which performs a step-by-step readout along the hierarchy of brain network informed by the brain atlas.

2 Method

An overview of our proposed HFBN-GCN is shown in Fig. 1. The whole architecture includes brain network construction, a topology-focused brain encoder, a hierarchical pooling module, and a multi-layer perceptron (MLP) to produce the final diagnosis.

2.1 Brain Functional Network Construction

The functional brain network is constructed from individual fMRI data. In the brain network with N nodes, each node represents an ROI, pre-defined by the Schaefer's atlas [14]. The connectivity matrix is denoted as A, with elements a_{ij} defining the FC between the i-th and the j-th ROIs. Following conventional studies, denote the s_i and s_j as the ROI-wise averaged BOLD signals from the i-th and the j-th ROIs, and $corr(si, sj)$ as their Pearson correlation defines the FC (a_{ij}).

2.2 Graph Convolutional Network

Graph Convolutional Network (GCN) is a popular implementation of Graph Neural Network (GNN), which generates the graph representation by integrating nodal features via the graph topology [9]. Besides the connectivity matrix, nodal features X are often required by GCN. In this study, we use the principal components yielded from FC matrix, by performing principal components analysis (PCA), as nodal features. The operation of GCN is defined as

$$X^{(l+1)} = \tilde{D}^{-\frac{1}{2}} \tilde{A} \tilde{D}^{\frac{1}{2}} X^{(l)} W \tag{1}$$

where $X^{(l)}$ denotes the feature map at the l-th layer, W is a matrix of learnable filter parameters and $\tilde{A} = A + I$, $\quad \tilde{D}_{ii} = \sum_j \tilde{A}_{ij}$.

It is worth noting that different GCN layers usually use the same topology of the graph, and generate node-level representations. So, in the tasks of graph-level classification, a readout function is necessary to generate whole-graph-level representation from all nodal level representations all at once [6] (Fig. 2).

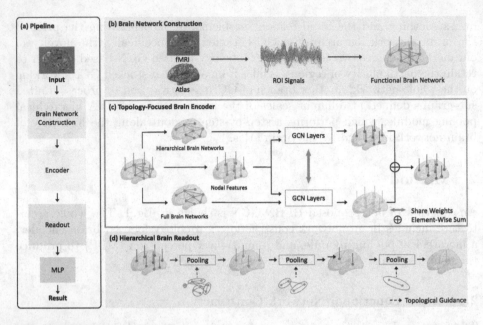

Fig. 1. The framework of HFBN-GCN. (a) The pipeline of the whole work. The functional brain network is constructed as an input to the encoder for extracting high-order graph feature representation. Then, a readout function is applied to aggregate features on all nodes. Finally, an MLP is used to produce the classification result. (b) fMRI data with an atlas produces ROI-wise averaged BOLD signals, used to construct functional brain network. (c) The nodal features will go through several GCN layers, in two paths, with the first path employing hierarchical topology and the second path utilizing the entire topology. (d) Features on all nodes are aggregated by several pooling layers, and the number of nodes is reduced step by step and finally integrated as an overall feature representation for the entire graph.

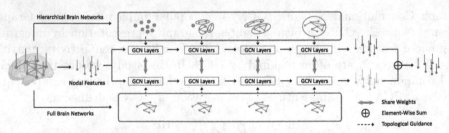

Fig. 2. The overview of our proposed topology-focused brain encoder.

2.3   Topology-Focused Brain Encoder

In general, in Eq. 1, $\tilde{D}^{-\frac{1}{2}}\tilde{A}\tilde{D}^{\frac{1}{2}}X^{(l)}$ denotes the progress of updating nodal features by averaging features from neighboring nodes. This message passing is overly simple, inevitably smoothing out nodal features after a few GCN layers [13]. It will also diminish the original heterogeneity of the nodes, such as hub vs. non-hub nodes, which may be crucial for brain disease diagnosis [15]. To alleviate this over-smoothing problem, we design message passing in our proposed hierarchical encoder to focus on sub-graphs defined by the brain hierarchy.

In this paper, we define 4 different levels of hierarchy, i.e., node level, hemispherical-7-network level, 7-network level [20], and whole brain level. At each level, we remove the FCs outside the sub-graphs, which leads to 4 adjacent matrices, $H^{(l)}, l = 1, 2, 3, 4$, with elements computed as

$$h_{ij}^{(1)} = 0 \quad \text{if } i \neq j, \tag{2}$$

$$h_{ij}^{(2)} = 0 \quad \text{if nodes } i, j \text{ not belonging to a same half-sub-network,} \tag{3}$$

$$h_{ij}^{(3)} = 0 \quad \text{if nodes } i, j \text{ not belonging to a same sub-network,} \tag{4}$$

$$h_{ij}^{(4)} = a_{ij}, \tag{5}$$

where $H^{(l)} = A$ before above operations. In this way, the message passing is thus restricted to the brain regions defined by each level.

However, the above defined operations diminish the long-range connections between regions/systems, which also causes information loss and the inappropriate graph encoding. To this end, we add another branch of GCNs to work on the original functional brain network, with the same number of layers as the branch that process the restricted functional brain network. The two feature maps generated by these two branches of GCNs are aggregated as the final features.

2.4 Hierarchical Brain Readout

In the graph-level classification task, the readout function, i.e., global pooling and reshaping [22], is usually applied to aggregate all node-level representations. However, such a global aggregation ignores the potential hierarchical nature of the graph. Weighted pooling method learns weights to aggregate nodes in an adaptive way, however, in common practice, the noise and bias in small data could yield an unreasonable pooling with the data-driven manner. Learning blindly without proper guidance is then not a solution.

To use the hierarchical pooling method and the prior from the atlas. We use a direct learnable assignment matrix P to cluster nodes. The process of clustering nodes can be given as

$$A^{(i+1)} = P^T A^{(i)} P, \tag{6}$$

$$X^{(i+1)} = P^T X^{(i)} \tag{7}$$

Also, to make the mapping relation follow biological-meaningful brain hierarchy, we further introduce a mask matrix $M \in \mathcal{R}^{N \times N'}$ to limit the clustering matrix, by

$$P \leftarrow M \circ P, \tag{8}$$

where ∘ denotes element-wise product, and $M_{ij} = 1$ means the i-th node will contribute to the j-th new node, otherwise $M_{ij} = 0$. Thus, the nodes belonging to one sub-network will not contribute to other sub-networks.

Consistently to the encoding process, we conducted the same 3 levels of pooling, but in a reversed order. Specifically, ROIs in the same sub-network of the same hemisphere are clustered together first, which means the shape of M in this pooling layer is 100×14 and $M_{ij} = 1$ if ROI i belong to half-sub-network j. Then the same sub-networks of both hemispheres are combined into an entire sub-network, and all sub-networks are finally grouped into a whole brain network.

3   Experiments

3.1   Dataset

We use a total of 910 fMRI data from 483 subjects in the Alzheimer's Disease Neuroimaging Initiative (ADNI2 and ADNIgo) [8].

Each fMRI scan includes 140 frames with temporal resolution of 3 s. The first 10 unstable frames are removed, and then fMRI data are pre-processed with a standard pipeline called AFNI [4], including slice timing correction, head motion correction, covariate removal, registration, band-pass temporal filtering (0.01–0.1 Hz), and spatial smoothing. In our experiments, we split the data randomly into a training set ($N_{NC} = 341, N_{eMCI} = 204$), a validation set ($N_{NC} = 110, N_{eMCI} = 71$), and a testing set ($N_{NC} = 114, N_{eMCI} = 70$). Note that all scans from the same subject are assigned to the same set.

3.2   Implementation

At the stage of brain functional network construction, one set of initial nodal features are 64 principal components yielded from its functional connectivity with other nodes. Eigenvectors are calculated in training data and applied to all data. All neural networks are implemented based on Pytorch, and trained with learning rate = 0.00005, epoch = 500, and batch size = 64. We use Adam as the optimizer. The loss function is set to a weighted cross entropy loss, and the class-specific weight are configured as 1 for HC and 1.5 for eMCI to ease the issue of sample unbalance between the two classes.

Encoder Module. *GCN*: The base network architecture is made up of an 8-layer GCN, a following max pooling layer for the readout, and a 2-layer MLP for generating the final prediction. The dimension of hidden layers are all 64. *GAT & FAGCN*: Graph Attention Networks (GAT) [16] and Frequency Adaptation Graph Convolutional Networks (FAGCN) [3] are two novel implementations of GNN, which introduce a learnable weight on the edge for modifying the message passing to alleviate the over-smoothing problem. In these two methods, we replace each GCN layer with a GAT or FAGCN layer in the baseline. *GCN with* *topology-focused brain encoder*: Compared to the baseline, an additional path using hierarchical topology is applied. The 4 different levels of hierarchy are defined in Eq. 5 and each of them contributes to 2 continuous GCN layers.

Readout Module. In this experiment, we keep the 8-layer GCN as an encoder and replace the readout functions from different methods. *GCN with weighted pooling*: Weighted summation on the whole-graph representation is used for readout. *GCN with hierarchal brain readout*: Our proposed readout processing is introduced above.

Effect of Choice of the Atlases. Yeo et al. [20] also provided a different atlas where the whole brain network is parcellated into 17 subnetworks. We thus implement a model with the 17-subnetwork atlas to investigate the effect of the choice of atlases. In this experiment, we use both proposed topology-focused brain encoder and hierarchical pooling.

3.3 Comparison of Methods

We perform the following comparisons to demonstrate the effectiveness of our proposed method. Classification accuracy, sensitivity, and specificity are computed to evaluate the performance of each method Table 1.

Table 1. Classification results of all competing methods (metrics reported in percentage). The underline indicates the highest metrics within same experiment, and the bold highlights the highest metrics among all methods.

Method	Accuracy	Sensitivity	Specificity
GCN	66.85	60.00	71.05
GAT	69.02	62.86	**72.81**
FAGCN	69.02	65.71	71.05
GCN w/ topology-focused Brain Encoder	70.65	68.57	71.93
GCN w/ Weighted Pooling	68.48	65.71	70.18
GCN w/ Hierarchical Pooling	71.74	72.86	71.05
HFBN-GCN (17-sub-network)	72.28	71.43	**72.81**
HFBN-GCN (7-sub-network)	**73.37**	**77.14**	71.05

Encoder Comparisons. Since GAT, FAGCN, and our topology-focused brain encoder focus on dealing with the over-smoothing problem, they all make an effort to keep the difference of nodes, and provide higher accuracy than the baseline. Additionally, our topology-focused brain encoder is slightly better than the other two methods, attributing to the utilization of prior knowledge.

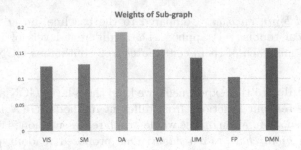

Fig. 3. Contributions of the functional sub-networks in the eMCI identifications. The full name of the 7 sub-networks: Visual (VIS), Somatomotor (SM), Dorsal Attention (DA), Ventral Attention (VA), Limbic (LIM), Frontoparietal (FP), and Default Mode Network (DMN).

Readout Comparisons. Then, we evaluate our proposed hierarchical brain readout. Compared to max pooling and weighted pooling, our method provides the best results in all metrics. Weighted pooling only blindly learns a hierarchy on the whole brain level and gives a medium level of accuracy, suggesting that priori knowledge can guide our hierarchical pooling module to cluster nodes in an effective way.

Fully Model and Effects of Atlas Setting. Finally, our proposed method, HFBN-GCN (7-sub-network), uses both topology-focused brain encoder and hierarchical pooling, leading to the best classification accuracy of 73.37%. In addition, we expect performance of the proposed method can rely on the prior hierarchy of brain network. Thus, we also investigate a model using the hierarchy of 17-sub-network [14]. It achieves an accuracy of 72.28%, slightly lower than our case of using the hierarchy of the 7-sub-network, but still shows the efficiency of our method in terms of accuracy when compared to other methods.

Predictive Contributions of Functional Sub-networks. Additionally, we extract weights on each functional sub-network from the final pooling layers of the best model (HFBN-GCN with 7-sub-network), which suggests contributions of each sub-network on eMCI identification tasks. Figure 3 shows that our network regards Dorsal Attention, Ventral Attention and Default Mode networks as the top 3 contributing sub-networks, where the first two are related to attention ability and the later one is associated with executive functions. This observation is in line with the findings in eMCI studies [11,17], which supports the interpretability of our proposed method.

4   Conclusion

We propose HFBN-GCN, a GCN-based architecture based on the hierarchical functional brain network for eMCI diagnosis. We design a topology-focused brain encoder to enhance nodal features from hierarchical functional network to alleviate the over-smoothing issue. Then we design a hierarchical brain readout to utilize pre-defined hierarchical information to guide the coarse-to-fine readout process. Experimental results on the ADNI dataset demonstrate the effectiveness of our proposed framework. Additionally, our method suggests the decisive functional sub-networks for eMCI identifications, which is in line with other eMCI studies.

References

1. Achard, S., Bullmore, E.: Efficiency and cost of economical brain functional networks. PLoS Comput. Biol. **3**(2), e17 (2007)
2. Betzel, R.F., Bassett, D.S.: Multi-scale brain networks. Neuroimage **160**, 73–83 (2017)
3. Bo, D., Wang, X., Shi, C., Shen, H.: Beyond low-frequency information in graph convolutional networks. arXiv preprint arXiv:2101.00797 (2021)
4. Cox, R.W.: AFNI: software for analysis and visualization of functional magnetic resonance neuroimages. Comput. Biomed. Res. **29**(3), 162–173 (1996)
5. Ghanbari, M., et al.: A new metric for characterizing dynamic redundancy of dense brain chronnectome and its application to early detection of Alzheimer's disease. In: Martel, A.L., et al. (eds.) MICCAI 2020. LNCS, vol. 12267, pp. 3–12. Springer, Cham (2020). https://doi.org/10.1007/978-3-030-59728-3_1
6. Gilmer, J., Schoenholz, S.S., Riley, P.F., Vinyals, O., Dahl, G.E.: Neural message passing for quantum chemistry. In: International Conference on Machine Learning, pp. 1263–1272. PMLR (2017)
7. Han, Y., et al.: Frequency-dependent changes in the amplitude of low-frequency fluctuations in amnestic mild cognitive impairment: a resting-state fmri study. Neuroimage **55**(1), 287–295 (2011)
8. Jack Jr., C.R., et al.: Magnetic resonance imaging in Alzheimer's disease neuroimaging initiative 2. Alzheimer's Dementia **11**(7), 740–756 (2015)
9. Kipf, T.N., Welling, M.: Semi-supervised classification with graph convolutional networks. arXiv preprint arXiv:1609.02907 (2016)
10. Langa, K.M., Levine, D.A.: The diagnosis and management of mild cognitive impairment: a clinical review. Jama **312**(23), 2551–2561 (2014)
11. Li, H.J., Hou, X.H., Liu, H.H., Yue, C.L., He, Y., Zuo, X.N.: Toward systems neuroscience in mild cognitive impairment and Alzheimer's disease: a meta-analysis of 75 fMRI studies. Human Brain Mapp. **36**(3), 1217–1232 (2015)
12. Norman, L.J., et al.: Structural and functional brain abnormalities in attention-deficit/hyperactivity disorder and obsessive-compulsive disorder: a comparative meta-analysis. JAMA Psychiatry **73**(8), 815–825 (2016)
13. Nt, H., Maehara, T.: Revisiting graph neural networks: all we have is low-pass filters. arXiv preprint arXiv:1905.09550 (2019)
14. Schaefer, A., et al.: Local-global parcellation of the human cerebral cortex from intrinsic functional connectivity MRI. Cereb. Cortex **28**(9), 3095–3114 (2018)
15. Van Den Heuvel, M.P., et al.: Abnormal rich club organization and functional brain dynamics in schizophrenia. JAMA Psychiatry **70**(8), 783–792 (2013)
16. Veličković, P., et al.: Graph attention networks. arxiv preprint arxiv:1710.10903 (2017)

17. Wu, H., et al.: An activation likelihood estimation meta-analysis of specific functional alterations in dorsal attention network in mild cognitive impairment. Front. Neurosci. **16** (2022)
18. Xing, X., et al.: Dynamic spectral graph convolution networks with assistant task training for early MCI diagnosis. In: Shen, D., et al. (eds.) MICCAI 2019. LNCS, vol. 11767, pp. 639–646. Springer, Cham (2019). https://doi.org/10.1007/978-3-030-32251-9_70
19. Xu, W., et al.: Altered functional connectivity of the basal nucleus of Meynert in subjective cognitive impairment, early mild cognitive impairment, and late mild cognitive impairment. Front. Aging Neurosci. **13** (2021)
20. Yeo, B.T., et al.: The organization of the human cerebral cortex estimated by intrinsic functional connectivity. J. Neurophysiol. (2011)
21. Zhang, D., Huang, J., Jie, B., Du, J., Tu, L., Liu, M.: Ordinal pattern: a new descriptor for brain connectivity networks. IEEE Trans. Med. Imaging **37**(7), 1711–1722 (2018)
22. Zhao, K., et al.: A dynamic graph convolutional neural network framework reveals new insights into connectome dysfunctions in ADHD. NeuroImage **246**, 118774 (2022)

Bayesian Filtered Generation of Post-surgical Brain Connectomes on Tumor Patients

Joan Falcó-Roget[(✉)] and Alessandro Crimi

Sano – Centre for Personalised Computational Medicine,
Czarnowiejska 36 building C5, 30-054 Kraków, Poland
j.roget@sanoscience.org

Abstract. Graph representation learning methods have recently been applied to predict how brain functional and structural networks will evolve in time. However, to obtain minimally coherent predictions, these methods require large datasets that are rarely available in sensitive settings such as brain tumors. Because of this, the problem of plasticity reorganization after tumor resection has been largely neglected in the machine learning community despite having an enormous potential for surgical planning. We present a machine learning model able to predict brain graphs following brain surgery, which can provide valuable information to surgeons planning better surgery. We rely on the idea that surgical outcomes share network similarities with healthy subjects and combine them in a Bayesian approach. We show how our method significantly outperforms simpler models even when taking advantage of the same prior. Furthermore, generated brain graphs share topological features with the real brain graphs. Overall, we present the problem of plasticity reorganization after brain surgery in a normative manner while still achieving competitive results.

Keywords: Graph generation · Surgical planning · Brain tumor

1 Introduction

Structural connections might be the source upon which functional activity and behavior rely on [27], but the relationship between structural and functional connections remains, not surprisingly, an open problem [7]. The problem of structural plasticity evolution is therefore a key step towards understanding the impact of disruptions and recovery in both the structural and functional connectomes in a variety of scenarios. In the present work, we tackle the problem of longitudinal structural connectivity prediction in brain networks recovering from surgical tumor resections using a cohort of healthy connectomes as a prior. Providing a prediction of how a human connectome will look like after tumor resection and recovery can provide insights to surgeons for better planning.

Remarkably, a great deal of effort has been put into the design of generative models of functional networks; however, the same cannot be said about structural

© The Author(s), under exclusive license to Springer Nature Switzerland AG 2022
L. Manfredi et al. (Eds.): ISGIE 2022/GRAIL 2022, LNCS 13754, pp. 79–88, 2022.
https://doi.org/10.1007/978-3-031-21083-9_8

connectomes. In this direction, a first approach considered an average of healthy networks at different time points to guide which connections should evolve [11]. Later, some studies [13,21] were able to use an adversarial generative model to improve the results using a large cohort of healthy connectomes.

The sensitivity of the pathologies in this study makes complicated the availability of sufficiently large and longitudinal datasets needed to train the data-hungry models discussed before. On top of that, we are not interested in predicting the temporal evolution of a healthy network which, presumably, is expected to have smooth and slow changes in plasticity, but rather address the reorganization of the connections after the abrupt change that any surgery causes. Finally, a brain tumor as well as its removal, critically affect parts of the network which might be far away from the damaged region itself [31], making the use of sufficiently detailed whole-brain networks necessary. In this regard, previous work relied on networks made of only 35 cortical ROIs making transfer learning an unfeasible approach while disregarding non-cortical lesions [8]. Altogether, and to best of our knowledge, these issues make our problem essentially un-studied. Nevertheless, we build on the idea that healthy networks should be used to inform and guide predictions. We propose to use them in a Bayesian framework in combination with simple yet robust machine learning models to produce detailed graphs that share both visual similarities and network measures with the ground truth.

2   Methods

Acquisition of MRIs. A detailed explanation of the participants as well as the acquisition of the data is already available [1,2]; nonetheless, for the sake of transparency we briefly present some crucial aspects. Subjects were asked to undergo MR scans both in pre- and post-surgery sessions. Out of the 36 subjects that agreed to take part in the pre-surgery session (11 healthy [58.6 ± 10.6 years], 14 meningioma [60.4 ± 12.3 years] and 11 glioma [47.5 ± 11.3 years]), 28 were scanned after a period spanning from 6 to 12 months in the post-surgery session (10 healthy [59.6 ± 10.3 years], 12 meningioma [57.9 ± 11.0 years] and 7 glioma [50.7 ± 11.7 years]). As a result, 19 pre- and post-surgery pairs of structural connectomes were usable as training and testing data. The majority of brain tumors were classified as grade I and II according to the World Health Organization. The healthy subjects were the partners of the patients matched by age, and with similar lifestyle [1,2].

Each MR session consisted of a T1-MPRAGE (voxel size of 1 mm^3) anatomical scan followed by a multi-shell (b = 0, 700, 1200, 2800 s/mm^2) HARDI acquisition together with two reversed phase-encoding b = 0 s/mm^2 blips for the purpose of correcting susceptibility-induced distortions [4].

Processing of MRIs and Network Reconstruction.   High resolution anatomical T1 weighted images were skull-stripped [16], corrected for bias field inhomogeneities [29], registered to MNI space [15] and segmented into 5 tissue-type images [24]. Diffusion weighted images suffer from many artifacts all of which were appropriately corrected. Images were also skull-stripped [16], corrected for susceptibility-induced distortions [4], denoised [30], freed from Gibbs ringing artifacts [18] and corrected for eddy-currents and motion artifacts [5]. The preprocessed images were then co-registered to its corresponding anatomical template (already in MNI space) [15], resampled to a 1.5 mm^3 voxel size and eventually corrected for bias field inhomogeneities [29]. After motion correction as well as registration to the MNI template, the B-matrix was appropriately rotated [19].

To ensure a detailed subject-specific network, we used a state-of-the-art pipeline to obtain the brain graphs. For each b-value shell and tissue type (white matter, gray matter and cerebrospinal fluid) a response function was estimated [10]. The fiber orientation distribution functions were built and intensity normalized using a multi-shell multi-tissue constrained spherical deconvolution approach [17]. Anatomically constrained probabilistic tractography (with 10M seeds and 3M streamlines) was performed using dynamic seeding [24]. To further improve correspondence between the tractograms and the preprocessed DWIs, we used spherical-deconvolution informed filtering [25]. The resulting tractographies were then compared to the third version of the Automated Anatomical Labeled atlas [22] to obtain a symmetric connectivity matrix between 166 brain regions for each subject.

Generation of Post-surgery Graphs with Artificial Neural Networks. We defined a connectome for the n-th subject at a particular time point t which, in our case, was mapped to control, pre- and post-surgery stages t_c, t_{pre} and t_{post}. Only the lower triangular part of the connectomes were flattened into a vector $\mathbf{x}_n(t)$ of E components, given that structural connections are always symmetric and no self-loops were considered. Each one of these components $x_{nk}(t)$ with $k = 1, \ldots, E$ represents a link of strength ϵ between two brain regions. We simplify the notation and refer to pre-surgery connectomes as $\mathbf{x}_n$, to post-surgery connectomes as $\mathbf{y}_n$ and to healthy connectomes as $\mathbf{z}_n$. We defined a distribution of binary links based on connectomes from N_C healthy subjects. For the k-th edge, $\lambda_k = 0, 1$ is a Bernoulli distributed binary variable with probability

$$P(\lambda_k = 1) = \frac{1}{N_C} \sum_{n=1}^{N_C} \Theta(z_{nk} - \theta) \tag{1}$$

where $\Theta(\cdot)$ is the Heaviside step function and $\theta = 0.2$ is a threshold that filters links with insufficient strength and therefore minimizing the false positive rate [9]. Lower thresholds allow more variability in the generated prior since more spurious connections can be considered. For each patient and edge, the post-surgery probability of having a meaningful link $\lambda_k = 1$ with strength ϵ is conditioned on the pre-operative graph. We exploit this fact with the well-known Bayes' theorem

$$P(y_{nk} = \epsilon, \lambda_k = 1 | \mathbf{x}_n) = \mathcal{L}(y_{nk} = \epsilon | \mathbf{x}_n) P(\lambda_k = 1) \tag{2}$$

where $\mathcal{L}(y_{nk} = \epsilon \mid \mathbf{x}_n)$ is the likelihood of having a post-surgery ϵ-strengthened connection conditioned on the pre-surgery connectome. For Eq. (2) to hold,

$P(\lambda_k = 1)$ must be independent on the pre-surgery graph $\mathbf{x}_n$. This assumption is reasonable since the anatomical prior was built using only healthy controls, therefore, not considering lesioned connections. We sampled each k-th connection using the Maximum A Posteriori criterion to generate the post-surgery graphs. To train the network, the sampled connections were then compared to the ground truth using the Mean Squared Error (MSE). Although many possibilities emerge for estimating the likelihood in Eq. (2), we used a fully connected network with one hidden layer. Several options were considered here, but we found that adding more layers or even considering 1D convolutions did not add significant improvements to the model.

Training and Testing. The high number of reconstructed fibers yielded high values for the connectivity between ROIs (10^3). To prevent numerical overflow as well as to enhance differences in lower connections, all weights ω were normalized by computing $log(1 + \omega)$ before feeding them into the artificial deep neural network.

The model consisted of a 1 hidden layer deep neural network which was trained minimizing the Mean Squared Error (MSE) between the output and the ground truth determined from the MRIs. Weights were optimized using stochastic gradient descent with a learning rate of 0.01 and 100 epochs to avoid overfitting. Evaluation metrics included the Mean Absolut Error (MAE), Pearson Correlation Coefficient (PCC) and the Cosine Similarity (CS) between the flattened predicted and ground truth graphs. The topology of the generated networks was evaluated computing the Kullback-Leiber as well as the Jensen-Shannon divergences between the weight probability distributions of the generated and real graphs.

Leave One Out cross validation was done using 18 connectomes to train each one of the 19 models. For each model, the training data was randomly split into train (80%) and validation (20%) sets to prevent overfitting. Validation steps were run every 20 training epochs. For each fold, the testing of each model was done in the left-out connectome. Statistical tests were done with Scipy's stats module. Topological metrics were computed using the Networkx python library [14]; averaged results are reported.

3 Results

Structural Predictions After Tumor Resection. Unfortunately, benchmarking against the models mentioned in the introduction [11,13,21], or similar ones, was not possible because they were not trainable with this small dataset. Previous work showed that linear models could capture essential properties of structural graphs [3]. Consequently, we proposed to evaluate a Fully Connected NETwork (FCNET) against a Huber Regressor and a null model. A Huber Regressor relies on a robust to outliers training scheme making it appealing when dealing with highly heterogenous data. Null models provide a way to avoid circular analysis in neuroscience [23]. As such, we also benchmarked FCNET against an untrained linear generator. For reproducibility, both the outputs of the Huber and ER generators were weighted by the same anatomical prior as the FCNET. For each model and fold, we tested the left-out network with 6 different metrics. The results for each score are in Table 1 for the mean and standard deviation.

FCNET significantly outperforms the null model in all evaluation metrics ($p < 0.001$, one sided t-test; $p < 0.001$ one sided U-test). When tested against the Huber regressor, FCNET significantly outperformed it in all the metrics assessing numerical similarities ($p < 0.05$, one sided t-test; $p < 0.05$ one sided U-test). However, when tested for topological accuracy, FCNET did not achieve any improvement with respect to the Huber regressor measured by the Kullback-Leibler (KL) and Jensen-Shanon (JS) divergences ($p > 0.31$, one sided t-test; $p = 0.24$, one sided U-test). Despite not being trained on preserving topological features, both FCNET and Huber captured structural properties since both models significantly decreased the KL ($p < 0.001$, one way ANOVA; $p < 0.001$ Kruskal-Wallis test) and JS ($p < 0.001$, one way ANOVA; $p < 0.001$ Kruskal-Wallis test) Divergences of the weight probability distributions between predicted and ground truth networks.

The training did not include a regularization method to prevent negative connections. However, FCNET generated negative connections accounted for less than 25% and they were all between 0 and -0.5. Since these values are in logscale they would account for a connection of less than 1 probably getting filtrated by the anatomical threshold. The generated post-surgery networks and residuals of two randomly selected subjects in Fig. 1.

Specific Subject Tunned Predictions. Brain networks are notoriously heterogeneous specially when it comes to brain tumors. The imposed anatomical prior, acted as a regularization method. However, a highly restrictive prior resulted in a complete loss of subject specificity despite FCNET achieving lower reconstruction errors. After some trial an error we found that an optimal (or nearly optimal) prior was able to discard enough connections while still capturing some inter-subject variability of the networks (Fig. 1 red squares). However, the model generalization does not allow for a perfect fit to the data, therefore a systematic error was present and observable in the residuals between the generated and ground truth networks (Fig. 1 right column).

Next, we asked whether FCNET was simply overfitting a small subset of similar subjects. We calculated the zscore of each metric with respect to the 19 folds cross validated subjects. For all metrics, we found that approximately 70%

Table 1. Model results (mean ± SEM). The Fully Connected NETwork (FCNET) was tested using a Leave One Out cross validation scheme in 6 metrics.

Model	MSE	MAE	PCC	CS	KL	JS
FCNET	**0.61 ± 0.02**	**0.49 ± 0.01**	**0.892 ± 0.004**	**0.922 ± 0.003**	8.19 ± 0.14	0.66 ± 0.01
HUBER	0.66 ± 0.03	0.52 ± 0.01	0.878 ± 0.005	0.914 ± 0.004	**8.09 ± 0.11**	**0.65 ± 0.01**
NULL	4.59 ± 0.07	1.22 ± 0.02	−0.00 ± 0.01	−0.00 ± 0.01	13.42 ± 0.04	0.82 ± 0.02

Connection Strength

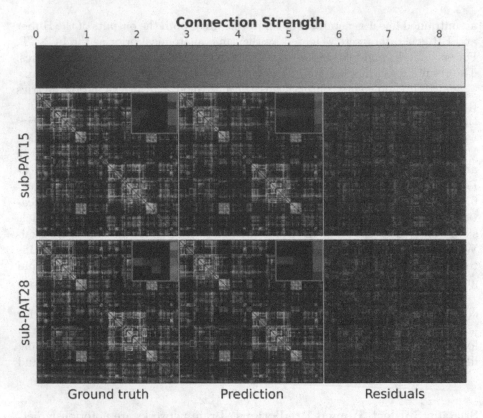

Fig. 1. FCNET's network generation. Two subjects were randomly selected to be displayed as a visual proof that FCNET captures essential properties of the post-surgery graphs. The residuals show the absolute difference between the predicted and ground truth networks. Negative connections were dropped for visualization purposes since they crucially affected the color scale but not the structure. FCNET can capture some specific inter-subject variabilities (augmented red squares) despite being trained on highly heterogeneous data. Connection strength is measured as $log\,(1+\omega)$ where ω is the native connectivity derived from the tractograms (Color figure online).

of all zscores lied in the $\pm\sigma$ range and approximately 95% fell in the $\pm2\sigma$. Even more, when repeating the training with different starting weights, all subjects but 2 showed different scores. These two subjects, however, had very different tumor morphologies pointing to the existence of confounding factors.

Topological Accuracy. We tested the topology of the generated networks by computing the weight probability distribution. The loss function used to train all models did not have any topological term, but generated networks shared global properties with the ground truth as measured by the KL and JS divergences in Table 1. The generated graphs showed a biological weight distribution with a small number of highly connected nodes (Fig. 2).

4 Discussion

In this work we presented a Fully Connected NETwork (FCNET) model to predict how brain connectomes will (or most probably) reorganize after the resection of the tumor. Our dataset consisted of 19 pairs of pre-/post-surgery graphs with 166 nodes. For each network, a total 13695 normalized edges needed to be reconstructed, thus making the problem ill-posed. Nonetheless, we hypothesized that a fully connected network adequately guided with anatomical information could capture some essential properties (both numerical and topological). We evaluated the model using Leave One Out Cross Validation therefore training and testing a total of 19 models or 19 folds. When tested against an alternative and null models, FCNET significantly outperformed them in all numerical scores, while still improving in the topological similarities with respect to the null model.

Anatomically Guided Network Generation. Brain tumors display high heterogeneity including size, location, histology, grade and infiltration in gray matter areas amongst others. As such, brain networks suffering from them also show great variability (Fig. 1). Furthermore, when undergoing surgery, there is no guarantee that all patients will react in the same way, therefore adding another source of complexity when understanding and predicting brain networks in unhealthy settings.

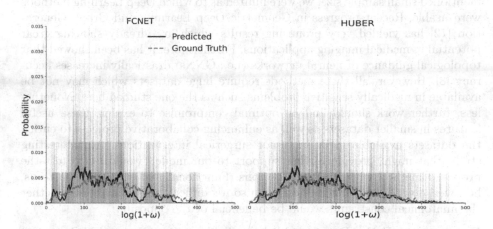

Fig. 2. Topological Accuracy. Black thick lines show the mean weight probability distribution predicted by FCNET (LEFT) and the HUBER regressor (RIGHT). Dashed red line shows the mean weight probability distribution of the real post-surgery graphs. Shaded background bars show the predicted distributions for each subject in the dataset. (Color figure online)

Previous work [11,13,21] suggested that guiding predictions with networks from healthy subjects achieved good results. As such, we designed a flexible

anatomical prior that was used to filter unplausible connections. Brain graphs
are notoriously heterogeneous when considering age related differences. To take
this into account, we selected healthy subjects with significant age overlapping
with patients in both tumor types. However, we did not consider gender segre-
gation since structural differences are rather unclear [20]. Since this age-specific
prior was backpropagated during the training phase, highly plausible connections were given more important when minimizing the loss function while, at
the same time, successfully discarding improvable edges. Furthermore, earlier,
studies on network topology found slight structural differences between healthy
and lesioned subjects [2,31], but these differences completely disappeared after
tumor resection [1], suggesting that self-organization naturally increases the similarity with healthy connections. In fact, surgical procedures aim to remove the
brain tumor without compromising in excess the rest of the tissue, therefore
justifying the use of healthy networks as a prior distribution for the model.

FCNET Surgical Outcomes. We used Leave One Out cross validation to test
FCNET's prediction against an alternative [3] and null models. FCNET significantly outperformed both when assessing numerical similarities. In contrast to
the alternative model, FCNET was able to both generalize and still capture some
inter-subject specificity (Fig. 1).

Limitations and Future Directions. The small size of the dataset allows and
invites for further repetitions of the results showed. Moreover, due to the afore
mentioned small sample size, we were limited as to which Deep Learning methods
were usable. Recent progress in Geometric Deep Learning and Graph Generation [12] has yielded very promising results which are already showing great
potential in medical imaging applications. Furthermore, it has been showed that
topological guidance of neural networks (i.e., GNNs) drastically increases accuracy [8]. However, all these methods require huge datasets which may not be
available in medically sensitive problems such as the one studied here. Nonetheless, further work should find an optimal compromise to exploit these useful
features in smaller datasets as well as enhancing collaborative projects to enrich
the datasets available in brain tumor surgerical interventions. An interesting
study that might provide further support to our model, would be to test the
proposed method with functional graphs. Functional and structural patterns,
however, do not share much in common so it's difficult to speculate on whether
the anatomical constraints would be beneficial or the opposite.

Dataset and Code. Data is publicly available at OpenNeuro ('BTC_preop',
'BTC_postop'). Processing of MRIs used several softwares [6,26,28]. Computa-
tions took 15 min in a NVIDIA GeForce GTX 3080 Ti GPU. *GitHub*

Acknowledgement. This research was supported by European Union's Horizon 2020
program [Sano No 857533] and by the Foundation for Polish Science [Sano project].

References

1. Aerts, H., et al.: Modeling brain dynamics after tumor resection using the virtual brain. NeuroImage **213**, 116738 (2020)
2. Aerts, H., et al.: Modeling brain dynamics in brain tumor patients using the virtual brain. Eneuro **5** (2018)
3. Aktí, Ş., et al.: A comparative study of machine learning methods for predicting the evolution of brain connectivity from a baseline timepoint. J. Neurosci. Methods **368**, 109475 (2022)
4. Andersson, J.L.R., Skare, S., Ashburner, J.: How to correct susceptibility distortions in spin-echo echo-planar images: application to diffusion tensor imaging. NeuroImage **20**, 870–888 (2003)
5. Andersson, J.L.R., Sotiropoulos, S.N.: An integrated approach to correction for off-resonance effects and subject movement in diffusion MR imaging. NeuroImage **125**, 1063–1078 (2016)
6. Avants, B.B., Tustison, N., Song, G., et al.: Advanced normalization tools (ANTS). Insight J. **2** (2009)
7. Avena-Koenigsberger, A., Misic, B., Sporns, O.: Communication dynamics in complex brain networks. Nat. Rev. Neurosci. **19**, 17–33 (2018)
8. Bessadok, A., Mahjoub, M.A., Rekik, I.: Brain multigraph prediction using topology-aware adversarial graph neural network. Med. Image Anal. **72**, 102090 (2021)
9. Collin, G., Kahn, R.S., de Reus, M.A., Cahn, W., van den Heuvel, M.P.: Impaired rich club connectivity in unaffected siblings of schizophrenia patients. Schizophrenia Bull. **40**, 438–448 (2014)
10. Dhollander, T., Raffelt, D., Connelly, A.: Unsupervised 3-tissue response function estimation from single-shell or multi-shell diffusion MR data without a coregistered T1 image. In: ISMRM Workshop on Breaking the Barriers of Diffusion MRI, vol. 5. ISMRM (2016)
11. Ezzine, B.E., Rekik, I.: Learning-guided infinite network atlas selection for predicting longitudinal brain network evolution from a single observation. In: Shen, D., et al. (eds.) MICCAI 2019. LNCS, vol. 11765, pp. 796–805. Springer, Cham (2019). https://doi.org/10.1007/978-3-030-32245-8_88
12. Faez, F., Ommi, Y., Baghshah, M.S., Rabiee, H.R.: Deep graph generators: a survey. IEEE Access **9**, 106675–106702 (2021)
13. Gürler, Z., Nebli, A., Rekik, I.: Foreseeing brain graph evolution over time using deep adversarial network normalizer. In: Rekik, I., Adeli, E., Park, S.H., Valdés Hernández, M.C. (eds.) PRIME 2020. LNCS, vol. 12329, pp. 111–122. Springer, Cham (2020). https://doi.org/10.1007/978-3-030-59354-4_11
14. Hagberg, A.A., Schult, D.A., Swart, P.J.: Exploring network structure, dynamics, and function using NetworkX. In: Proceedings of the 7th Python in Science Conference (2008)
15. Jenkinson, M., Bannister, P., Brady, M., Smith, S.: Improved optimization for the robust and accurate linear registration and motion correction of brain images. NeuroImage **17**, 825–841 (2002)
16. Jenkinson, M., Pechaud, M., Smith, S., et al.: BET2: MR-based estimation of brain, skull and scalp surfaces. In: Eleventh Annual Meeting of the Organization for Human Brain Mapping, Toronto, vol. 17, p. 167 (2005)
17. Jeurissen, B., Tournier, J.D., Dhollander, T., Connelly, A., Sijbers, J.: Multi-tissue constrained spherical deconvolution for improved analysis of multi-shell diffusion MRI data. NeuroImage **103**, 411–426 (2014)

18. Kellner, E., Dhital, B., Kiselev, V.G., Reisert, M.: Gibbs-ringing artifact removal based on local subvoxel-shifts. Magn. Resonance Med. **76**, 1574–1581 (2016)
19. Leemans, A., Jones, D.K.: The B-matrix must be rotated when correcting for subject motion in DTI data. Magn. Resonance Med. **61**, 1336–1349 (2009)
20. Luders, E., Kurth, F.: Structural differences between male and female brains (2020)
21. Nebli, A., Kaplan, U.A., Rekik, I.: Deep EvoGraphNet architecture for time-dependent brain graph data synthesis from a single timepoint. In: Rekik, I., Adeli, E., Park, S.H., Valdés Hernández, M.C. (eds.) PRIME 2020. LNCS, vol. 12329, pp. 144–155. Springer, Cham (2020). https://doi.org/10.1007/978-3-030-59354-4_14
22. Rolls, E.T., Huang, C.C., Lin, C.P., Feng, J., Joliot, M.: Automated anatomical labelling atlas 3. NeuroImage **206**, 116189 (2020)
23. Rubinov, M.: Circular and unified analysis in network neuroscience. OSF PrePrints (2022)
24. Smith, R.E., Tournier, J.D., Calamante, F., Connelly, A.: Anatomically-constrained tractography: improved diffusion MRI streamlines tractography through effective use of anatomical information. NeuroImage **62**, 1924–1938 (2012)
25. Smith, R.E., Tournier, J.D., Calamante, F., Connelly, A.: SIFT: Spherical-deconvolution informed filtering of tractograms. NeuroImage **67**, 298–312 (2013)
26. Smith, S.M., et al.: Advances in functional and structural MR image analysis and implementation as FSL. NeuroImage **23**(Suppl. 1), S208–S219 (2004)
27. Suárez, L.E., Markello, R.D., Betzel, R.F., Misic, B.: Linking structure and function in macroscale brain networks. Trends Cognit. Sci. **24**, 302–315 (2020)
28. Tournier, J.D., et al.: MRtrix3: a fast, flexible and open software framework for medical image processing and visualisation. NeuroImage **202**, 116137 (2019)
29. Tustison, N.J., et al.: N4ITK: improved N3 bias correction. IEEE Trans. Med. Imaging **29**, 1310–1320 (2010)
30. Veraart, J., Fieremans, E., Novikov, D.S.: Diffusion MRI noise mapping using random matrix theory. Magn. Resonance Med. **76**, 1582–1593 (2016)
31. Yu, Z., et al.: Altered brain anatomical networks and disturbed connection density in brain tumor patients revealed by diffusion tensor tractography. Int. J. Comput. Assist. Radiol. Surg. **11**, 2007–2019 (2016)

Deep Cross-Modality and Resolution Graph Integration for Universal Brain Connectivity Mapping and Augmentation

Ece Cinar, Sinem Elif Haseki, Alaa Bessadok, and Islem Rekik[✉] iD

BASIRA Lab, Faculty of Computer and Informatics Engineering, Istanbul Technical University, Istanbul, Turkey
irekik@itu.edu.tr
http://basira-lab.com/

Abstract. The connectional brain template (CBT) captures the shared traits across all individuals of a given population of brain connectomes, thereby acting as a fingerprint. Estimating a CBT from a population where brain graphs are derived from diverse neuroimaging modalities (e.g., functional and structural) and at different resolutions (i.e., number of nodes) remains a formidable challenge to solve. Such network integration task allows for learning a rich and universal representation of the brain connectivity across varying modalities and resolutions. The resulting CBT can be substantially used to generate entirely new multimodal brain connectomes, which can boost the learning of the downs-stream tasks such as brain state classification. Here, we propose the Multimodal Multi-tiresolution Brain Graph Integrator Network (i.e., M2GraphIntegrator), *the first multimodal multiresolution graph integration framework that maps a given connectomic population into a well-centered CBT.* M2GraphIntegrator first unifies brain graph resolutions by utilizing resolution-specific graph autoencoders. Next, it integrates the resulting fixed-size brain graphs into a universal CBT lying at the center of its population. To preserve the population diversity, we further design a novel clustering-based training sample selection strategy which leverages the most heterogeneous training samples. To ensure the biological soundness of the learned CBT, we propose a topological loss that minimizes the topological gap between the ground-truth brain graphs and the learned CBT. Our experiments show that from a single CBT, one can generate realistic connectomic datasets including brain graphs of varying resolutions and modalities. We further demonstrate that our framework significantly outperforms benchmarks in reconstruction quality, augmentation task, centeredness and topological soundness.

Keywords: Connectional brain templates · Multi-modal multi-resolution integration · Data augmentation · Graph neural network

1 Introduction

Modern network science opens new frontiers of representing the complex functionality and structure of biological systems by analyzing the intercommunication within

---

E. Cinar and S.E. Haseki—Co-first authors.

L. Manfredi et al. (Eds.): ISGIE 2022/GRAIL 2022, LNCS 13754, pp. 89–98, 2022.
https://doi.org/10.1007/978-3-031-21083-9_9

their fundamentals [1]. The wealth of technological advances in the field of neuro-science paves the way for gathering massive and high-quality biological datasets such as Human Connectome Project [2], Southwest University Longitudinal Imaging Multi-modal (SLIM) Brain Data Repository [3] and UK Biobank [4] using different magnetic resonance imaging (MRI) modalities including functional, structural T1-weighted and diffusion MRI. Representing such connectomic datasets using graphs (i.e., networks) aims to reveal the complex interconnections between brain regions. More specifically, each brain graph allows to investigate particular connectivity patterns and functional-ities of the brain elements, where each anatomical brain region of interest (i.e., ROI) is represented with a node and the biological connectivity between two ROIs is rep-resented by weighted edges [5–7]. Using graphs that are derived from such rich mul-timodal datasets serves as an exemplary tool for examining the human brain structure and state [8,9] by mapping the brain wiring at the *individual* level.

In addition to fingerprinting the brain of an individual, graph representations allow for mapping brain connectivity at the *population* level, thereby distinguishing between contrasting states (e.g., healthy versus unhealthy) of different populations. Emerging studies focused on learning how to integrate a set of unimodal single-resolution brain graphs into a single connectome (i.e., connectional brain template) that encodes the shared traits across the individuals of the population [10–12]. Despite their overwhelm-ing success, existing methods [13] are not particularly designed to handle *multimodal multiresolution* connectomic datasets, which, if solved, can pave the way for holisti-cally detecting anomalies and abnormalities across varying brain networks. Specifically, generating a universal connectional brain template (i.e., CBT) from a *multimodal mul-tiresolution connectomic population* remains an uncharted territory [13]. By mitigating such a challenging issue, a single compact representation, from which one can span new multimodal multiresolution brain graph populations for data augmentation [14,15], can be learned to reveal typical and atypical alterations in the brain connectome across modalities and various individuals. One can also leverage the universal CBT for *graph augmention* to alleviate clinical data scarcity [14,16–18] in classification and regression tasks [19–23].

Related Work. Existing works tailored for graph integration or fusion in general are limited to training on unimodal, single-resolution brain networks [10–12,24]. For exam-ple, based on message passing between the neighbors of a particular node, similarity network fusion (SNF) [24] learns how to integrate a set of biological graphs by dif-fusing the local connectivity of each individual graph across the global connectivity of all samples in the population in an iterative manner. Still, such method cannot handle multiresolution graphs as well as heterogeneous samples drawn from multimodal dis-tributions. Later on, [10] proposed a novel method for estimating a CBT (also termed with brain network atlas) over a population of brain networks which are derived from the same modality by exploiting diffusive-shrinking and fusing graph techniques. How-ever, the mathematical formalization of the proposed graph diffusion and fusion method is not capable of handling multigraph population, where each sample is represented by a set of graphs. To remedy the lack of methods for *multigraph data integration*, where a multigraph allows for multiple edges connecting two nodes, [11] introduced a novel approach for multi-view graph construction. However, such method utilizes disparate learning modules that learn independently without any feedback mechanism between them; as such the errors accumulate throughout the dichotomized learning pipeline. To address this issue, [12] introduced Deep Graph Normalizer (DGN) framework, the first graph neural network that integrates a population of fixed-size multigraphs in an end-to-end learnable way. Although compelling, DGN is limited to aggregating the information only across multi-view brain graphs with a *fixed resolution*. Besides, it relies on a random sampling technique to generate CBTs, which is agnostic to *data heterogeneity*. Moreover, DGN uses edge-conditioned convolution, which is not fundamentally tailored for easing the memory consumption, thereby undermining the population representative CBT estimation for large-scale graph populations. Other related works [25, 26] focused only on integrating single-resolution brain network populations for disorder profiling and CBT learning. We note a few works that were also dedicated to brain graph super-resolution [27–29], which primarily aimed to generate brain graphs across different resolutions rather then integrating them.

To address all these limitations, we propose *Multimodal Multiresolution Graph Integrator* (M2GraphIntegrator) Network, the first framework for integrating a population of *multimodal multi-resolution* brain networks into a centered and representative CBT. Tapping into the nascent field of GNNs, we design a set of resolution-specific autoencoders to map a given population of brain networks of different resolutions derived from multiple modalities to a shared embedding space. Next, given the learned embeddings, we generate the CBT through the integrator network, which is an architecture specialized in learnable embedding integration. To train our framework, we design a novel CBT *centeredness loss* that ensures the heterogeneity of training samples via clustering. As such, the selected training samples from different clusters represent each and every distribution present in the input graph population. In that way, our estimated CBT can capture the connectivity patterns across all subjects in a diverse population. Furthermore, to preserve the brain graph topology in the integration process, we propose a novel *topology loss* which aims to minimize the topological gap between the ground truth and the reconstructed brain graphs in terms of node strength, a measure quantifying the local hubness of each brain node (i.e., anatomical region of interest).

2 Proposed Method

In this section, we present the main steps of our CBT estimation framework from multimodal multi-resolution brain networks. Figure 1 provides an overview of the key three steps of the proposed framework: **A)** representation of multimodal and multi-resolution brain networks in a population, **B)** generation of subject-based CBT, **C)** subject-specific loss calculation, and **D)** estimation of the universal CBT.

A- Multi-modal Multi-resolution Brain networks Representation. Given a connectomic population, each subject is represented by multiple brain networks of different resolutions derived from different neuroimaging modalities such as functional and structural MRI (Fig. 1-**A**). Such brain networks do not necessarily belong to the same resolution set (i.e., they might have different number of nodes thus different number of edges). Therefore, we represent each subject s in the population as follows:

$$\mathcal{X}_s = \{X_s^m\}_{m=1}^M, \quad X_s^m = \{\mathbf{X}_s^{m,r_k}\}_{k=1}^{K^m}, \text{ where } r_1 < \cdots < r_k < \cdots < r_{K^m}$$

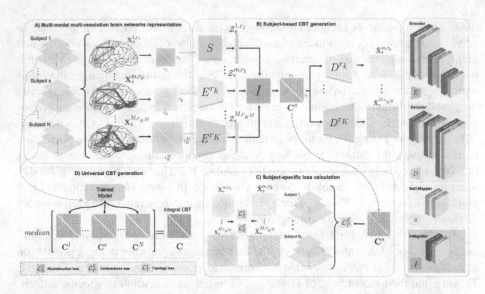

Fig. 1. *Overview of the proposed Multi-modal Multi-resolution Graph Integrator (M2GraphIntegrator) architecture for estimating a centered connectional brain template from a given population.* (**A**) **Multi-modal multi-resolution brain network representation.** We represent each subject in the population by multiple connectivity matrices, each denoted by $\mathbf{X}_s^{m,r_k} \in \mathbb{R}^{r_k \times r_k}$. (**B**) **Subject-based CBT generation.** Our framework consists of 3 co-learning modules: the resolution-specific graph autoencoders, the self-mapper and the integrator. We generate the subject-based CBT by integrating the feature vector embeddings $\mathcal{Z}_s^{m,r_k}$ of each encoder and the self-mapper. (**C**) **Subject-specific loss calculation.** For each subject s, we calculate both reconstruction and topological losses using the whole training set. As for the CBT centeredness loss, using clustering we select a heterogeneous subset of training samples against which we evaluate the centeredness of the learned subject-specific CBT. (**D**) **Universal CBT generation**. To capture the most centered connectional patterns across all subjects, we feed each brain multigraph through our trained model to generate subject-based CBTs. Next, we perform element-wise median operation to estimate the *universal CBT*. To simplify the illustration, we denote the encoder $E^{r_K^M}$ by E^{r_K} and $D^{r_K^M}$ by D^{r_K}.

X_s^m denotes the modality-specific brain networks set derived from modality m and $\mathcal{X}_s$ stands for the overall set encapsulating each and every modality-specific brain networks set of subject s. $\mathbf{X}_s^{m,r_k} \in \mathbb{R}^{r_k \times r_k}$ represents a connectivity matrix (i.e. adjacency matrix) of resolution r_k belonging to X_s^m. We represent the total number of resolutions derived from modality m by K^m and further denote by K the total number of resolutions across all modalities. Since each connectivity matrix is symmetric, we vectorize it into a feature vector by taking the elements in its lower triangular part. Specifically, for each subject, we represent each brain graph with a feature vector $\mathbf{V}_s^{m,r_k} \in \mathbb{R}^{1 \times r_k'}$, where $r_k' = \frac{r_k \times (r_k-1)}{2}$. We note in what follows that our GCN is trained in a subject-based fashion where each subject is represented by a single-node brain graph.

B-Subject-Based CBT Generation. To estimate a subject-based CBT $\mathbf{C}^s$, we design 3 GCN-based modules that co-learn during the training process: the *resolution-specific graph autoencoders*, the *self-mapper* and the *integrator* (Fig. 1-**B**).

Resolution-Specific Graph Encoder. In order to generate a subject-based CBT, we first propose to reduce the resolution of differently scaled brain networks. To do so, we introduce a set of resolution-specific graph encoders $\{E^{r_k}\}_{k=2}^K$, where each E^{r_k} maps the feature vectors of a network at resolution r_k into a shared lower embedding space at the lowest existing graph resolution r_1. Our encoders learn to capture the shared-traits across multi-resolution brain networks. We build the encoders by stacking three GCN blocks each including a GCN layer followed by sigmoid non-linearity and a dropout function. Each GCN layer performs the graph convolution operation [30] defined as follows: $\mathbf{V}^l = \hat{\mathbf{D}}^{-1/2}\hat{\mathbf{A}}\hat{\mathbf{D}}^{-1/2}\mathbf{V}^{l-1}\Theta^l$, where $\mathbf{V}^l$ denotes the feature vector embedding at layer l, $\hat{\mathbf{D}}$ denotes the diagonal degree matrix, $\hat{\mathbf{A}}$ denotes the adjacency matrix including self-connectivities and Θ^l denotes the learnable parameter for each layer l. For simplicity, we choose $\mathbf{V}$ as a representation of $\mathbf{V}_s^{m,r_k}$ which is the feature vector of a subject s with a resolution r_k and modality m. We note that feature vector embedding of the last layer (i.e., third layer of E^{r_k}) is denoted by $\mathcal{Z}$ where $\mathcal{Z} = \mathbf{V}^L$ (i.e., feature vector embedding at layer L, where $L = 3$ in our case).

As the first step of estimating $\mathbf{C}^s$, we pass the feature vectors of subject s each denoted by $\mathbf{V}_s^{m,r_k}$ through their corresponding resolution-specific graph encoders in order to map them to the shared embedding space of size r_1'. We represent the low-dimensional embedding of each feature vector by $\mathcal{Z}_s^{m,r_k} \in \mathbb{R}^{1 \times r_1'}$. We note that the minimal resolution brain graphs of subject s are passed to another architecture called the *self-mapper*, which we will detail in the following section.

Self-mapper. The self-mapper is an architecture aiming to generate feature vector embeddings which capture the shared-traits across subjects of a given population. It maps minimal-resolution feature vectors into the embedding space shared among the resolution-specific graph encoders. Since the self-mapper does not alter the resolution of its input feature vectors, it cannot be identified as an encoder. However, the self-mapper and resolution-specific graph encoders resemble each other in terms of generating population-representative feature vector embeddings. The self-mapper consists of a single GCN block built by stacking a GCN layer, sigmoid non-linearity and dropout function and is denoted by S throughout our framework (Fig. 1-B). In line with the purpose of estimating $\mathbf{C}^s$, we pass each minimal-resolution feature vector $\mathbf{V}_s^{m,r_1}$ of subject s through the self-mapper and denote their embeddings by $\mathcal{Z}_s^{m,r_1}$.

Integrator. We introduce an integrator module I to integrate the feature embeddings $\mathcal{Z}_s^{m,r_k}$ generated by the different resolution-specific graph encoders $\{E^{r_k}\}_{k=2}^K$ and the self-mapper S into a single representation –i.e., the *subject-based* CBT. It mainly encapsulates multiple integration blocks, each composed of a linear layer followed by sigmoid non-linearity. Mainly, to estimate $\mathbf{C}^s$ we first pass feature embeddings of subject s through their corresponding integration blocks. Second, we average the integration block outputs and generate the subject-based CBT $\mathbf{C}^s$ in its vectorized version (Fig. 1-B). Finally, we derive the matrix representation of $\mathbf{C}^s$ by simple antivectorization.

Resolution-Specific Graph Decoder. We design our M2GraphIntegrator framework in a way that each resolution-specific graph encoder E^{r_k} has a corresponding resolution-specific graph decoder denoted by D^{r_k}. These encoder-decoder pairs are symmetric since both architectures consist of identical graph convolutional blocks in a reversed order. Even though decoders are not directly involved in the subject-based CBT estimation process, they play a substantial role in the overall framework by forcing the encoders, the self-mapper and the integrator to better learn the population graph representation. To achieve this, we propose two losses: the *reconstruction loss* and the *topology loss* which we will address in the following sections. Specifically, each decoder D^{r_k} maps the learned $\mathbf{C}^s$ into a higher embedding space of size r_k in order to reconstruct the initial feature vector of subject s, which is antivectorized into the reconstructed brain connectivity matrix $\hat{\mathbf{X}}_s^{m,r_k}$. We note that our resolution-specific graph decoders can be further leveraged for **multimodal brain network data augmentation** by perturbing the learned population CBT.

C- Subject-Specific Loss Calculation. Once we generate $\mathbf{C}^s$ from the integrator, we calculate a *centeredness loss* inspired by the subject normalization loss (SNL) proposed in [12]. However, SNL cannot preserve the data heterogeneity of the population which might result in a limited representation that fails to fully capture the spectrum of brain connectivity variability across subjects. To solve this problem, we propose a different method for selecting a subset $\mathcal{D}_S$ of our training dataset $\mathcal{D}$. Specifically, we employ a clustering-based sampling method (e.g., K-means or hierarchical clustering) rather than solely using random sampling. For *centeredness loss* calculation, we first vectorize the input connectivity matrices and stack the resulting feature vector embeddings. Next, to select a $\mathcal{D}_S$, we employ a clustering step to sample subjects from different clusters and produce their embedding vectors $\mathcal{Z}_s^{m,r_k}$ using the encoder E^{r_k}. Finally, we obtain $\mathbf{Z}_s^{m,r_k}$ by antivectorizing $\mathcal{Z}_s^{m,r_k}$ for each sample in $\mathcal{D}_S$ and calculate the mean Frobenius distance (MFD) with respect to $\mathbf{C}^s$: $\mathcal{L}_P^s = \sum_{m=1}^M \sum_{k=1}^{K^m} \sum_{n=1}^{N_S} ||\mathbf{C}^s - \mathbf{Z}_s^{m,r_k}||_2^2$. To ensure that the decoded network preserves the initial traits present in the ground-truth graphs, we introduce a *reconstruction loss* which computes the MFD between the ground-truth connectivity matrices $\mathbf{X}_s^{m,r_k}$ and their reconstructed matrices $\hat{\mathbf{X}}_s^{m,r_k}$ for each subject s. We define it as follows: $\mathcal{L}_R^s = \sum_{m=1}^M \sum_{k=1}^{K^m} ||\mathbf{X}_s^{m,r_k} - \hat{\mathbf{X}}_s^{m,r_k}||_2^2$. We further propose a new *topology loss* to enforce the connectivity strength of the brain regions in the reconstructed brain graphs $\hat{\mathbf{X}}_s^{m,r_k}$ to be similar to those of the ground-truth networks $\mathbf{X}_s^{m,r_k}$. More specifically, we generate for each subject in the population $\hat{\mathbf{X}}_s^{m,r_k}$ by passing the vectorized $\mathbf{C}^s$ through the decoder D^{r_k}. Next, we calculate the node strength vectors $\mathbf{P}_s^{m,r_k}$ and $\hat{\mathbf{P}}_s^{m,r_k}$ by summing up then normalizing over the rows of $\mathbf{X}_s^{m,r_k}$ and $\hat{\mathbf{X}}_s^{m,r_k}$, respectively. Hence, we define it as follows: $\mathcal{L}_T^s = \sum_{m=1}^M \sum_{k=1}^{K^m} ||\mathbf{P}_s^{m,r_k} - \hat{\mathbf{P}}_s^{m,r_k}||_1$. By combining the three sub-losses (Fig. 1-C), we define the total subject-specific loss for a training subject s as follows:

$$\mathcal{L}_J^s = \sum_{m=1}^M \sum_{k=1}^{K^m} \Big(\underbrace{||\mathbf{X}_s^{m,r_k} - \hat{\mathbf{X}}_s^{m,r_k}||_2^2}_{\text{Reconstruction loss}} + \lambda_1 \underbrace{||\mathbf{P}_s^{m,r_k} - \hat{\mathbf{P}}_s^{m,r_k}||_1}_{\text{Topology loss}} + \lambda_2 \underbrace{\sum_{n=1}^{N_S} ||\mathbf{C}^s - \mathbf{Z}_n^{m,r_k}||_2^2}_{\text{Centeredness loss}} \Big)$$

In that way, our proposed loss not only captures the topological structure and information of different networks, but also the shared traits across subjects of the population.

D- Universal CBT Generation. Since our ultimate goal is to generate a population representative CBT rather than a subject-based CBT, we further propose an additional step in our framework. Since each $\mathbf{C}^s$ generated in the previous step is biased by a particular subject, we need to acquire a centered CBT that represents the heterogeneous population. To mitigate this issue, we perform element-wise median operation on all generated subject-based CBTs (i.e., $\mathbf{C}^s$) as follows: $\mathbf{C} = median[\mathbf{C}^1, \mathbf{C}^2, ..., \mathbf{C}^N]$, where N represents the number of training subjects (Fig. 1-**D**). As a result, we estimate $\mathbf{C}$ the integral CBT that represents each and every subject in a multimodal multi-resolution brain graph population.

3   Results and Discussion

Connectomic Dataset and Hyperparameter Setting. We trained and tested our framework on a connectomic dataset derived from the Southwest University Longitudinal Imaging Multimodal (SLIM) Brain Data Repository [3]. The dataset consists of 279 young healthy subjects, each represented by two brain networks of resolutions (i.e., ROIs) 35 and 160 derived from T1-weighted (morphological network) and resting-state functional MRI (functional network). We benchmarked our **M2GraphIntegrator** including the topological loss (**T**) with its two (**K**) K-means and (**H**) hierarchical clustering variants against four ablated versions: **Ablated (K)** and **Ablated (H)** employ K-means and hierarchical clustering without integrating the topology loss while **Ablated (R+T)** and **Ablated (R)** employ random sampling with and without including the topology loss, respectively. We initialized two clusters for each clustering-based sampling method and selected 10 training subjects at each epoch. Prior to calculating the population *centeredness loss*, we provided an extra training of 100 epochs for the resolution-specific graph autoencoder architecture to achieve more reliable and steady results in the graph reconstruction block. We used grid search to tune the hyperparameters λ_1 and λ_2 of our loss function $\mathcal{L}_j^s$ and set them to 2 and 0.5, respectively. We used Adam optimizer and set the learning rate to 0.0001.

Evaluation of Universal CBT Centeredness and Topological Soundness. A representative CBT lies at the center of its population, hence it needs to achieve the minimal distance to all subjects in the population. We first use 5-fold cross-validation to split the data into training and testing folds where the CBT is learned from the training set and evaluated against the unseen test set. To evaluate the centeredness of the universal CBT, we first encode the testing functional graphs with 160×160 resolution by the trained E^{160}. Next, we compute the mean Frobenius distance between the CBT matrix learned from the training set and each morphological and encoded functional matrix of testing subjects. Next, to assess the topological soundness of the estimated CBT, we compute the Euclidean distance between their corresponding node strength representations. Lower values of the centeredness and topological soundness measures demonstrate that the generated CBT is more representative and topology-aware. Table 1 shows the significant outperformance of our M2GraphIntegrator across all evaluation measures using both K-means and hierarchical clustering methods. Notably, these results show that our model learned using the proposed topology loss function significantly outperforms ($p < 0.01$) the comparison methods in preserving the topological properties of the ground-truth networks.

Table 1. *CBT evaluation results using different measures.* Centeredness and topological soundness evaluate the quality of the generated CBT. KL divergence and pairwise distance evaluate the ability of the learned CBT in generating sound multimodal brain networks at different resolutions for data augmentation. For each metric, we highlight in bold the best performing method and underline the second best. Both M2GraphIntegrator (K+T) and (H+T) significantly outperformed ablated comparison methods ($p - value < 0.01$ using two-tailed paired t-test). **K**: K-means clustering. **H**: hierarchical clustering. **R**: random sampling. **T**: topological loss.

Model Variation	Evaluation Measure			
	Centeredness	Top. Soundness	KL Divergence	Pairwise Dist.
Ablated (R)	19.0727	5.9825	0.9764	0.1495000
Ablated (K)	19.0702	5.9767	0.9766	0.1495006
Ablated (H)	19.0755	5.9831	0.9765	0.1495009
Ablated (R+T)	17.9822	5.8448	0.7245	0.1421824
M2GraphIntegrator (K+T)	<u>17.9819</u>	<u>5.8439</u>	**0.7241**	<u>0.1421812</u>
M2GraphIntegrator (H+T)	**17.9783**	**5.8434**	<u>0.7243</u>	**0.142180**

Evaluation of Multimodal Network Augmentation from the Learned Universal CBT. Assuming that the *universal CBT* spans all domains across modalities and resolutions, it can be easily utilized to generate new brain networks for potential downstream learning tasks (e.g., connectome regression [31]). First, we simulate 279 random networks of the same CBT size and distribution. Next, we regularize each random network by averaging it with the universal CBT. Next, we feed each average network to our resolution-specific graph decoders to generate multimodal networks. To assess the realness of the generated networks, we compute the Kullback-Leibler divergence [32] between the ground-truth and the augmented brain networks as well as their average pairwise Euclidean distance (Table 1). Hence, a lower result in both metrics represents higher similarity between the ground-truth and the networks generated from our *universal* CBT (Table 1). Remarkably, the universal CBT by our methods **M2GraphIntegrator (K+T)** and **M2GraphIntegrator (H+T)** generates more significantly ($p < 0.01$) realistic multimodal brain graphs compared to the benchmarks.

4   Conclusion

In this paper, we proposed Multi-modal Multi-resolution Graph Integrator which is the first graph neural network framework that estimates a connectome population fingerprint given *multimodal multi-resolution* brain networks. Our method has three compelling strengths: (i) the autoencoder learning task with joint multi-resolution GCN-based autoencoders, facilitating its customizability to any graph resolution, (ii) the design of the *clustering-based* training sampling in the centeredness loss computation to learn a well-representative CBT of the population heterogeneity and (iii) the proposal of the *topology loss* to estimate a topologically sound CBT. Our estimated CBTs will not only pave the way for easier brain disorder diagnosis by revealing deviations from the healthy population but also remedy data scarcity by augmenting new brain networks. In our future work, we will use our model to learn universal CBTs of various healthy and disordered brain connectivity datasets including functional, morphological, and structural connectomes. Besides, we will refine our architecture by integrating a novel graph new edge-convolution that operates on large-scale graphs without memory overloading.

Acknowledgements. This work was funded by generous grants from the European H2020 Marie Sklodowska-Curie action (grant no. 101003403, http://basira-lab.com/normnets/) to I.R. and the Scientific and Technological Research Council of Turkey to I.R. under the TUBITAK 2232 Fellowship for Outstanding Researchers (no. 118C288, http://basira-lab.com/reprime/). However, all scientific contributions made in this project are owned and approved solely by the authors.

References

1. Ideker, T., Galitski, T., Hood, L.: A new approach to decoding life: systems biology. Annu. Rev. Genomics Hum. Genet. **2**, 343–372 (2001)
2. Essen, D., et al.: The human connectome project: a data acquisition perspective. Neuroimage **62**, 2222–31 (2012)
3. Qiu, J., Qinglin, Z., Bi, T., Wu, G., Wei, D., Yang, W.: (Southwest university longitudinal imaging multimodal (SLIM) brain data repository: a long-term test-retest sample of young healthy adults in southwest china)
4. Biobank, U.: About UK biobank (2014). https://www.ukbiobank.ac.uk/about-biobank-uk
5. Fornito, A., Zalesky, A., Breakspear, M.: The connectomics of brain disorders. Nat. Rev. Neurosci. **16**, 159–172 (2015)
6. Fornito, A., Zalesky, A., Bullmore, E.: Fundamentals of Brain Network Analysis. Academic Press (2016)
7. van den Heuvel, M.P., Sporns, O.: A cross-disorder connectome landscape of brain dysconnectivity. Nat. Rev. Neurosci. **20**, 435–446 (2019)
8. Seidlitz, J., et al.: Morphometric similarity networks detect microscale cortical organization and predict inter-individual cognitive variation. Neuron **97**, 231–247 (2018)
9. Holmes, A.J., et al.: Brain genomics superstruct project initial data release with structural, functional, and behavioral measures. Sci. Data **2**, 1–16 (2015)
10. Rekik, I., Li, G., Lin, W., Shen, D.: Estimation of brain network atlases using diffusive-shrinking graphs: application to developing brains. In: Niethammer, M., Styner, M., Aylward, S., Zhu, H., Oguz, I., Yap, P.-T., Shen, D. (eds.) IPMI 2017. LNCS, vol. 10265, pp. 385–397. Springer, Cham (2017). https://doi.org/10.1007/978-3-319-59050-9_31
11. Dhifallah, S., Rekik, I., Initiative, A.D.N., et al.: Estimation of connectional brain templates using selective multi-view network normalization. Med. Image Anal. **59**, 101567 (2020)
12. Gurbuz, M.B., Rekik, I.: Deep graph normalizer: a geometric deep learning approach for estimating connectional brain templates. In: Martel, A.L., Abolmaesumi, P., Stoyanov, D., Mateus, D., Zuluaga, M.A., Zhou, S.K., Racoceanu, D., Joskowicz, L. (eds.) MICCAI 2020. LNCS, vol. 12267, pp. 155–165. Springer, Cham (2020). https://doi.org/10.1007/978-3-030-59728-3_16
13. Bessadok, A., Mahjoub, M.A., Rekik, I.: Graph neural networks in network neuroscience. arXiv preprint arXiv:2106.03535 (2021)
14. Nalepa, J., Marcinkiewicz, M., Kawulok, M.: Data augmentation for brain-tumor segmentation: a review. Front. Comput. Neurosci. **13**, 83 (2019)
15. Perl, Y.S., et al.: Data augmentation based on dynamical systems for the classification of brain states. Chaos, Solitons Fractals **139**, 110069 (2020)

16. Sserwadda, A., Rekik, I.: Topology-guided cyclic brain connectivity generation using geometric deep learning. J. Neurosci. Methods **353**, 108988 (2021)
17. Khan, A., Fraz, K.: Post-training iterative hierarchical data augmentation for deep networks. Advances in Neural Information Processing Systems 33 (2020)
18. You, Y., Chen, T., Sui, Y., Chen, T., Wang, Z., Shen, Y.: Graph contrastive learning with augmentations. Adv. Neural. Inf. Process. Syst. **33**, 5812–5823 (2020)
19. Perez, L., Wang, J.: The effectiveness of data augmentation in image classification using deep learning. arXiv preprint arXiv:1712.04621 (2017)
20. Mikołajczyk, A., Grochowski, M.:Data augmentation for improving deep learning in image classification problem. In: 2018 International Interdisciplinary PhD Workshop (IIPhDW). IEEE (2018) 117–122
21. Graa, O., Rekik, I.: Multi-view learning-based data proliferator for boosting classification using highly imbalanced classes. J. Neurosci. Methods **327**, 108344 (2019)
22. Wong, S.C., Gatt, A., Stamatescu, V., McDonnell, M.D.: Understanding data augmentation for classification: when to warp? In: 2016 International Conference on Digital Image Computing: Techniques and Applications (DICTA), pp. 1–6. IEEE (2016)
23. Du, Y., Fu, Z., Calhoun, V.D.: Classification and prediction of brain disorders using functional connectivity: promising but challenging. Front. Neurosci. **12**, 525 (2018)
24. Wang, B., et al.: Similarity network fusion for aggregating data types on a genomic scale. Nat. Methods **11**, 333 (2014)
25. Demir, U., Gharsallaoui, M.A., Rekik, I.: Clustering-based deep brain multigraph integrator network for learning connectional brain templates. Uncertainty for Safe Utilization of Machine Learning in Medical Imaging, and Graphs in Biomedical Image Analysis, pp. 109–120 (2020)
26. Sağlam, M., Rekik, I.: Multi-scale profiling of brain multigraphs by eigen-based cross-diffusion and heat tracing for brain state profiling. Uncertainty for Safe Utilization of Machine Learning in Medical Imaging, and Graphs in Biomedical Image Analysis, pp. 142–151 (2020)
27. Isallari, M., Rekik, I.: Gsr-net: graph super-resolution network for predicting high-resolution from low-resolution functional brain connectomes. In: International Workshop on Machine Learning in Medical Imaging, pp. 139–149 (2020)
28. Mhiri, I., Mahjoub, M.A., Rekik, I.: Stairwaygraphnet for inter-and intra-modality multi-resolution brain graph alignment and synthesis. In: International Workshop on Machine Learning in Medical Imaging, pp. 140–150 (2021)
29. Mhiri, I., Khalifa, A.B., Mahjoub, M.A., Rekik, I.: Brain graph super-resolution for boosting neurological disorder diagnosis using unsupervised multi-topology connectional brain template learning. Med. Image Anal. **65**, 101768 (2020)
30. Kipf, T.N., Welling, M.: Semi-supervised classification with graph convolutional networks (2017)
31. Shen, X., et al.: Using connectome-based predictive modeling to predict individual behavior from brain connectivity. Nature Protocols **12**, 506–518 (2017)
32. Kullback, S.: Information theory and statistics. Courier Corporation (1997)

Using Hierarchically Connected Nodes and Multiple GNN Message Passing Steps to Increase the Contextual Information in Cell-Graph Classification

Joe Sims[2,3]([✉]), Heike I. Grabsch[1,2], and Derek Magee[3]

[1] Department of Pathology, GROW School for Oncology and Reproduction,
Maastricht University Medical Center+, Maastricht, The Netherlands
[2] Pathology and Data Analytics, Leeds Institute of Medical Research at St. James's,
University of Leeds, Leeds, UK
scjps@leeds.ac.uk
[3] School of Computing, University of Leeds, Leeds, UK

Abstract. Graphs are useful in analysing histopathological images as they are able to represent neighbourhood interactions and spatial relationships. Typically graph nodes represent cells and the vertices are constructed by applying a nearest neighbor algorithm to cell's locations. When passing these graphs through one graph neural network (GNN) message passing step, each node can only utilise features from nodes within its immediate neighbourhood to make a classification. To overcome this, we introduce two levels of hierarchically connected nodes that we term "supernodes". These supernodes, used in conjunction with at least four GNN message passing steps, allow for cell node classifications to be influenced by a wider area, enabling the entire graph to learn tissue-level structures. The method is evaluated on a supervised task to classify individual cells as belonging to a specific tissue class. Results demonstrate that the inclusion of supernodes with multiple GNN message passing steps increases model accuracy.

Keywords: Graph neural network · Node classification · Digital pathology

1 Introduction

The phenotype and topological distribution of tissue components may influence cancer progression as well as patient prognosis and response to therapy [1, 2]. Convolutional neural networks (CNNs) have demonstrated to be effective at common computer vision tasks such as image classification and segmentation [3]. However, traditional CNNs only model local relations and are applied to data in a grid structure with fixed connectivity. When applying CNNs to patches from multi-gigabyte whole slide images (WSIs) this limits the model from learning wider representations and doesn't consider the interactions between entities within the tumour microenvironment. This paper tackles this issue by representing tissue as a graph structure which conserves spatial relations. We

L. Manfredi et al. (Eds.): ISGIE 2022/GRAIL 2022, LNCS 13754, pp. 99–107, 2022.
https://doi.org/10.1007/978-3-031-21083-9_10

augment the graphs with multiple levels of hierarchy to increase the radius of spatial context that each node can utilise.

Graphs inherently capture relationships between entities making them appropriate for representing the tumour microenvironment. Graph neural networks (GNNs) are a variation of deep learning that accept graphs as input. These GNNs are able to capture different neighbourhood relations and accept irregular sized inputs. Furthermore, they have shown comparable accuracies to CNNs when performing disease classification [4, 5], and tissue segmentation [6]. One subclass of GNNs is a graph attention network (GAT) [7] which leverages masked self-attention layers to learn different weights for specific nodes within a neighbourhood of arbitrary size.

Propagating a graph through a GNN once is often referred to as one message passing step. In one GNN message passing step, information from nodes one hop away influence the learnt node embeddings. With every additional T GNN message passing step, information from nodes T hops away influence the learnt node embeddings [8]. However, there is currently no guidance regarding the number of message passing steps required for 'optimal' learning of node representations, specifically when applied to hierarchical graphs.

Several approaches have been made to develop adequate tissue-representations using graphs and GNNs. Zhou, Y., et al. [4] captured the tumour cell microenvironment using cell-graphs (graphs whose nodes represent cells), while others have used a number of clustering methods to represent tissue-level structures [1, 5, 6]. However, independent of the graph formation method, whilst only using one GNN message passing step, learnt node embeddings will be limited to the influence of its immediate neighbours. P. Pati, et al. [1] suggested a hierarchical graph structure which introduced connectivity between cells and larger, non-overlapping tissue regions. Although this method was successful at increasing context and capturing multi-scale information, the number of nodes representing the tissue level structures in conjunction with only two GNN message passing steps, limits the context that can be learnt. Furthermore, there was no suggested method for introducing additional layers of hierarchical connections.

In P. Pati, et al. [1] and Anklin, V., et al. [6] node features were obtained by passing forward image patches through a pre-trained CNN to produce features that are abstract and exposed to bias arising from variability in colour and scanner-specific attributes across pathology slides [9]. Whereas, Zhou, Y., et al. [4] extracted morphological cell features which are independent of these biases.

In this paper, we propose a method that applies the concept of hierarchical graph formation to cell-graphs to increase the contextual information when learning tissue-level representations. We introduce two sets of sparsely distributed, regularly spaced nodes termed "supernodes" which form edge connections in a hierarchical manner. To produce an optimal result from these nodes, we can demonstrate that a GNN model's architecture should be composed of multiple (at least four) GNN message passing steps. The main contributions of this paper are:

- A novel method for creating hierarchical graphs that increases contextual information without being limited by the size of tissue regions or exposed to bias arising from variation across histopathology slides;

- The use of multiple, (at least four) independently-weighted GNN message passing steps to utilise the hierarchically connected supernodes within the graph;
- An evaluation of the proposed methods in a node classification task to segment tissue regions in 54 HE-stained cores containing tumour regions from patients with stage II/IIIb gastric cancer.

2 Method

2.1 Data

The dataset used in this paper was composed of 2 haematoxylin-eosin (HE) stained tissue-microarrays (TMAs) containing 54 3 mm diameter tissue cores sampled from tumour regions from patients with stage II/IIIb gastric cancer. Using the HeteroGenius MIM Cell-Analysis Add-On (HeteroGenius, Leeds, UK) which is a U-NET-based cell detector and classifier trained on over 50,000 annotated cells, the centroid position of every cell nucleus within the cores were detected along with 14 other features. These included size (μm), elongation, mean intensity, standard deviation of intensity, angle and the cell's probability of being one of the following cell types: tumour, lymphocyte, granulocyte, plasma cell, fibroblast, muscle, endothelium, normal epithelium, and other. Within the two TMAs this resulted in ~2.6 million cells detected with their 14 corresponding features.

The specific task this method was applied to was node classification to identify large tissue structures. Four output classes were identified with a pathologist. These classes were: cancer, muscle, stroma and follicle (aggregates of lymphocytes). Regions were manually annotated by a pathologist to define the ground truths. Roughly ~2.5% (~67,000) of the total cells were labelled. For each core, the cells were randomly assigned to a train-test split of 80% and 20%, respectively.

2.2 Cell-Graph Formation

A graph is defined as $G = (V, E)$ where V are a set of nodes (vertices) with corresponding features and E are the edges connecting two nodes. These have corresponding features that represent their interaction. To form the cell-graph, each cell was represented as a node. Assuming that cell interactions occur between adjacent cells, edge connections were formed by applying the k-d tree nearest-neighbor algorithm to all cell coordinates in the individual TMA cores, with k-neighbours $= 5$ and the number of leaf nodes set to n $= 3$.

2.3 Supernodes

To increase the context of a cell node's learnt embedding, we introduce two levels of hierarchically connected supernodes. To define the first level of supernodes (L1), a square grid of edge length 200 μm is superimposed onto the TMA core. The locations of the grid's vertices define the locations of the L1 supernodes. Edges are formed with every cell node and other L1 supernodes within a 200μm radius. The L1 supernode features are calculated as the average of the cell node features whom it shares an edge with.

For the second level of supernodes (L2), a square grid of edge length 400μm, aligned with the same coordinate space as the L1 grid, is superimposed onto the TMA core. The locations of this grid's vertices define the locations of the L2 supernodes. Edges are formed with every L1 supernode within a 200μm radius. Figure 1 provides a visualization of the locations of the two levels of supernodes and one set of hierarchically connected nodes.

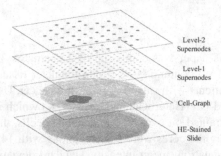

Fig. 1. A visualization of the supernodes' positions and an example of one L2 supernode and its hierarchical connections (connected nodes shown in red). The HE-stained slide is included for reference.

Introducing the supernodes significantly increases the number of edge connections. Across the 54 TMA cores, Table 1 shows the average number of cells, L1 supernodes, and L2 supernodes, as well as the number of cumulative edges as the supernodes are introduced. The number of edges includes shown in Table 1 includes self-loops.

Table 1. For each node type, the number of nodes and edges are the average over the 54 TMA cores. The number of edges include self-loops.

Node type	Number of nodes	Number of edges
Cell Nodes Only	30,205	85,899
Cell Nodes + L1	30,373	175,888
Cell Nodes + L1 + L2	30,416	176,224

2.4 Model Architecture

The method in this work uses a GAT with one attention head that contains a 2-layer feed forward neural network within one GNN message passing step. The feed forward network is shown in Eq. (1) where h_i is the set of input node features for the i-th node, h_i' is the corresponding transformed output, W_k are learnable sets of weights, and *tanh* is the hyperbolic tangent activation function. The activation function *tanh* was used over *LeakyReLU* due to its superior performance during experimentation.

The input node features had size 17 which consisted of the 14 output features from the HeteroGenius MIM cell-analysis tool along with a one-hot encoding of the node's supernode status. Cell nodes were encoded as [1,0,0], L1 supernodes as [0,1,0], and L2 supernodes as [0,0,1].

$$\vec{h}_i' = tanh\left(W_3 tanh\left(W_2 tanh\left(W_1 \vec{h}_i\right)\right)\right) \tag{1}$$

The input also included 3 edge features. These were: the difference in x-coordinates; the difference in y-coordinates; and the Euclidean distance between the source and target node. For all nodes, self-loops were included with edge features equal to 0.

The attention mechanism within the network was modified to account for edge features. In Eq. (2), the edge features e_{ij} corresponding to the edge connecting the i-th node and its j-th neighbor are concatenated with the transformed node features [10], where a is the attention weight vector and α_{ij} is the multi-head attention coefficient.

$$\alpha_{ij} = \frac{exp\left(LeakyRelu\left(\vec{a}^T\left[\vec{h}_i' \| \vec{h}_j' \| \vec{e}_{ij}\right]\right)\right)}{\sum_{k \in \mathcal{N}_i}\left(exp\left(LeakyRelu\left(\vec{a}^T\left[\vec{h}_i' \| \vec{h}_j' \| \vec{e}_{ij}\right]\right)\right)\right)} \tag{2}$$

Mentioned in Xu, K., et al. [11] and evident in Eq. (2), one GNN message passing step allows information from immediately connected neighbours (one hop away) to influence the i-th node's representation. To embed information from nodes T hops away, information would have to pass sequentially through T GNN message passing steps, where each message passing step is comprised of a new set of weights. This makes it unfeasible to embed distant information by stacking tens of message passing steps end-to-end as the number of parameters would either be too large to train, making it subject to computational limits or be subject to vanishing and exploding gradients. Furthermore, nodes that are tens of hops away would have negligible influence on node's learnt representations compared with nodes fewer hops away. However, by using two levels of supernodes in conjunction with multiple (four) GNN message passing steps, information is able to travel from one cell node up to a L2 supernode and back down to another cell node that exists a maximum distance of 800μm away. Figure 2 demonstrates this concept of information travelling from one cell node to a L1 and L2 supernode, then travelling back down to a separate L1 supernode and cell node, using four GNN message passing steps.

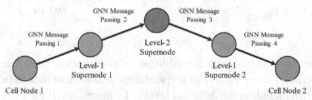

Fig. 2. Above shows how information from Cell Node 1 can be influence the learnt node embedding of Cell Node 2 by being passing information through 4 GNN message passing steps.

Although the GAT model allows for the implementation of multiple attention heads and the inclusion of a multi-layer feed forward network, both of which can increase the accuracy of the learnt representation, this would not achieve the same function as multiple GNN message passing steps. Increasing the number of attention heads and layers in the feed forward network would continue to aggregate information one hop away and not allow for the influence of nodes multiple hops away.

2.5 Experiential Evaluation

To assess the influence of supernodes on the learnt node representations and evaluate the effect of using multiple GNN message passing steps, two experiments were carried out. One was to assess how the addition of L1 supernodes and L2 supernodes influence the overall accuracy. The other was to assess how the number of GNN message passing steps influence the accuracy of the model when using two levels of supernodes. During training the loss function used was a masked, weighted MSE loss. Each model was trained for 10,000 epochs with a learning rate of 1e-3.

3 Results

3.1 The Inclusion of Supernodes

Firstly, all models used in this experiment had 4 GNN message passing steps. The node feature sizes from the input (17) to output (4) were 17, 64, 64, 64 and 4. For comparison, three models were trained and tested on the data containing different levels of hierarchy. Specifically the three sets of data were: cell nodes with no supernodes; cell nodes with L1 supernodes; and cell nodes with both L1 and L2 supernodes. No further cross validation was carried out. Table 2 shows the accuracy of the three models on the train and test sets.

Table 2. The model accuracy when trained and tested with and without the existence of supernodes. 'Node Type' represents the additional presence of the L1 and L2 supernodes.

Node type	Train accuracy	Test accuracy
Cell Nodes Only	73.66	73.15
Cell Nodes + L1	90.69	90.50
Cell Nodes + L1 + L2	**93.80**	**93.40**

It is clear in Table 2 that with the addition of supernodes, there was a significant increase in accuracy. Figure 3 provides a visual demonstration of how the model's output was affected when including the different levels of supernodes. Figure 3a) shows a clear presence of localized noise, and the classifications appear to be more locally clustered. Whereas, in Fig. 3c) larger scale structures such as tissue regions are evident, showing an increase in context in the learnt node embeddings.

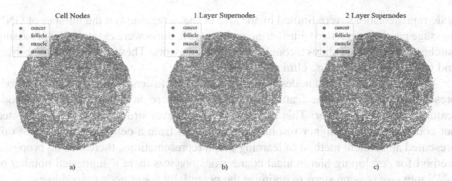

Fig. 3. An example of the model's outputs when trained on a) only the cell-graph, b) the cell-graphs with the inclusion of L1 supernodes, and c) the cell-graph with the inclusion of L1 and L2 supernodes

3.2 Multiple GNN Message Passing Steps

The second experiment was to determine how the number of GNN message passing steps influences the model's performance when used in conjunction with 2 levels of supernodes. Four models were trained for comparison. For each model, the number of input features were 17 and output features were 4. For models composed of >1 GNN message passing step, the intermediate node features were 64. These are shown in Table 3.

Table 3. The accuracy of the model composed of n message passing steps where $n = 1, 2, 3, 4$

Number of Message Passing Steps	Node Features	Train Accuracy	Test Accuracy
1	17, 4	72.77	73.15
2	17, 64, 4	89.38	88.12
3	17, 64, 64, 4	90.31	90.50
4	17, 64, 64, 64, 4	**93.80**	**93.40**

The results in Table 3 suggest that increasing the number of GNN message passing steps increases the accuracy when applied to hierarchical graphs containing two levels of supernodes.

4 Discussion

P. Pati, et al. [1] introduced applying hierarchically connected nodes to histopathology slides. They determined nodes as the centres of tissue regions that were connected to cells lying within those tissue regions. This was demonstrated to be effective at increasing context in a graph classification task. However, no method was proposed for further increasing the context through more hierarchical connections. As a result, the learnt node representations were limited by the size of tissue regions and the number of GNN message passing steps (two). Furthermore, the node features were extracted from passing patches of HE-stained slides through a pretrained network. These features were abstract and uninterpretable with no clinical context.

W. Lu, et al. [5] defined nodes as the centres of cell clusters. Similarly to the methods presented in this work, the features of these nodes were an average of the cell node features within the cluster. This allowed for tissue-level structures to be represented but could not capture higher resolution information from a cellular level. Whilst this presented an efficient method of learning graph representations, there was no proposed method for developing hierarchical connections nor was there a suggested number of GNN message passing steps to optimize the potentially learnt node embeddings.

The method proposed in this paper allows for the representation of granular information from the cells and provides a method for creating indefinite levels of hierarchically connected nodes that we termed "supernodes". These supernodes have shown to increase context in a node classification task, allowing for tissue-level structures to be learnt on a cellular level. We demonstrate that to optimize the outcomes from using two levels of supernodes, multiple (at least four) GNN message passing steps are required.

When comparing the number of message passing steps, it is likely that the increase in performance seen in Table 2 was a result of including more learnable parameters. However, we demonstrated that with the inclusion of 2 levels of hierarchically connected supernodes, this number of GNN message passing steps enabled the graph to learn from an increased context. In addition, the model accuracy is high ($>90\%$) and only considered 17 input node features, all of which held clinical relevance.

One limitation of this work lies in the labelled output classes. With the tumour-microenvironment being complex and heterogeneous [8, 12], in many scenarios there are more than four tissue classes. Likewise, these tissue regions don't consistently maintain hard boundaries which makes the assignment of a single class subjective and inconsistent. However, this was not inherent to the model but to the labelling system. A further limitation lies within the quantity of annotated data ($\sim$2.5% of all cell nodes). This is significantly lower than that proposed in Gao, J.P., et al. [8] who demonstrated the effect of incomplete labels on a graph-based segmentation task, with the lowest percentage of annotated data covering 5% of the total pixels within the tissue.

5   Conclusion

In this paper, we have presented a novel method for increasing the contextual information when performing node classification on cell-graphs containing tumour regions. We introduced the concept of supernodes that can be connected hierarchically. From comparing the accuracy of models trained on cell nodes alone, cell nodes with one level of supernodes, and cell nodes with two levels of supernodes, we can conclude that the inclusion of supernodes increases the contextual information learnt by cell nodes. Through a separate comparison, the accuracy was compared between four models composed of 1–4 GNN message passing steps. The model with 4 GNN message passing steps achieved the highest performance implying that this architecture is required to utilise two levels of supernodes.

References

1. Pati, P., et al.: Hierarchical graph representations in digital pathology. Med. Image Anal. **75**, 102264 (2022)
2. Mi, H., et al.: Digital pathology analysis quantifies spatial heterogeneity of CD3, CD4, CD8, CD20, and FoxP3 immune markers in triple-negative breast cancer. Front. Physiol. **11**, 583333 (2020)
3. Janowczyk, A., Madabhushi, A.: Deep learning for digital pathology image analysis: a comprehensive tutorial with selected use cases. J. Pathol. Inform. **7**, 29 (2016)
4. Zhou, Y., et al.: CGC-net: cell graph convolutional network for grading of colorectal cancer histology images. In: 2019 IEEE/CVF International Conference on Computer Vision Workshop (ICCVW) (2019)
5. Lu, W., et al.: Capturing cellular topology in multi-gigapixel pathology images. In: 2020 IEEE/CVF Conference on Computer Vision and Pattern Recognition Workshops (CVPRW) (2020)
6. Anklin, V., et al.: Learning whole-slide segmentation from inexact and incomplete labels using tissue graphs (2021). arXiv:2103.03129
7. Veličković, P., et al.: Graph attention networks (2017). arXiv:1710.10903
8. Gao, J.P., et al.: Tumor heterogeneity of gastric cancer: from the perspective of tumor-initiating cell. World J. Gastroenterol. **24**(24), 2567–2581 (2018)
9. Anghel, A., et al.: A high-performance system for robust stain normalization of whole-slide images in histopathology. Front. Med. (Lausanne) **6**, 193 (2019)
10. Chen, J., Chen, H.: Edge-featured graph attention network (2021). arXiv:2101.07671
11. Xu, K., et al.: Representation learning on graphs with jumping knowledge networks (2018). arXiv:1806.03536
12. Junttila, M.R., de Sauvage, F.J.: Influence of tumour micro-environment heterogeneity on therapeutic response. Nature **501**(7467), 346–354 (2013)

TaG-Net: Topology-Aware Graph Network for Vessel Labeling

Linlin Yao[1,2], Zhong Xue[1], Yiqiang Zhan[1], Lizhou Chen[4], Yuntian Chen[4], Bin Song[4], Qian Wang[3(✉)], Feng Shi[1], and Dinggang Shen[1,3]

[1] Shanghai United Imaging Intelligence Co., Ltd., Shanghai, China
[2] Institute for Medical Imaging Technology, School of Biomedical Engineering, Shanghai Jiao Tong University, Shanghai, China
[3] School of Biomedical Engineering, ShanghaiTech University, Shanghai, China
wangqian2@shanghaitech.edu.cn
[4] Department of Radiology, West China Hospital, Sichuan University, Chengdu, China

Abstract. Anatomical labeling of head and neck vessels is a vital step for cerebrovascular disease diagnosis. However, it remains challenging to automatically and accurately label vessels in computed tomography angiography (CTA), since head and neck vessels are tortuous, branched, and often close to nearby tubular-like vasculatures. To address these challenges, we transform the voxel labeling problem into the centerline labeling task and propose a novel method of topology-aware graph network (TaG-Net) for vessel labeling of 18 segments covering both head and neck, in which the efficiency of centerline' sparse representation using the point cloud is exploited and vessel's topological structure can be better represented using the topology-aware graph. First, a topology-aware graph is constructed from the extracted vessel centerlines. Second, we design topology-preserving sampling and topology-aware feature grouping so that the network's sampling and grouping layers preserve the vascular structures. Third, the vascular features extracted from the point processing layer and the GCN layer are aggregated for centerline labeling. Finally, the labeling task is accomplished by assigning the closet label from each point of the centerline to the mask voxels. Using head and neck CTA of 401 subjects and a five-fold-cross-validation strategy, experiments show that TaG-Net yields an average recall of 0.977 and an average precision of 0.977, with mean F1 as 0.977 for centerline labeling. After back-propagating labels onto vessel masks, TaG-Net achieves an average Dice coefficient of 0.991 for 18 vessel segments compared to that of 0.980 by the V-Net. The results indicate that the proposed network could facilitate head and neck vessel analysis by providing automatic and accurate vessel labeling.

Keywords: Head and neck vessels · Anatomical labeling · Topology-aware graph

L. Manfredi et al. (Eds.): ISGIE 2022/GRAIL 2022, LNCS 13754, pp. 108–117, 2022.
https://doi.org/10.1007/978-3-031-21083-9_11

1   Introduction

Vascular diseases are the leading cause of death globally and are often associated with high morbidity and medical risks [5]. Computed Tomography Angiography (CTA) is the major imaging modality in diagnosing vascular diseases, and CTA in head and neck is usually used for examining carotid and vertebral arteries and blood vessels within the brain. In automated vessel analysis, after segmenting the vessel masks, it is of great interest to label each anatomical segment so that abnormalities can be localized and visualized along with a selected pathway for convenient reading and diagnosis. For example, centerlines with proper labels not only provide an intuitive visualizing region of a segment's straightened lumen for radiologists but also facilitate localization and quantification of stenosis and calcification within the blood vessels. Automated labeling is also a prerequisite step for generating reports in a computer-aided diagnosis (CAD) system.

In the literature, a number of works have been proposed for labeling coronary arteries [2,14,16,18], brain arteries [1,3,4,12,13], and head and neck arteries [17]. In [14], Wu *et al.* utilizes a registration-based method so that the vessel structure from the atlas can be used as prior knowledge for labeling new data. A logic rule-based refinement is needed for this no-data-driven method. Other registration-based methods include [1,13] for brain arteries, which may not adapt to large shape variability among individuals and the tortuous structures of arteries. TreeLab-Net [14] uses the topological structures such as position features extracted from a centerline as the input for labeling each vessel segment. However, the algorithm neglects the graph property of the vessel tree. CPR-GCN [16] combines the features extracted from the TreeLab-Net and the graph information learned from a graph convolutional network (GCN), while considering three-dimensional image features. However, the graph down-sampling method used in GCN does not preserve graph topology. Chen *et al.* developed a GNN approach to label ICA with hierarchical refinement (HR) on the Intracranial artery. HR was conducted to address the problem of global structures and relations learning existing in the GNN. In [4], Hampe *et al.* constructed a coronary artery tree graph based on the connectivity between the centerlines. Then this tree graph was transformed into a linegraph. At last, a graph attention network was applied on the linegraph to label the segments. On the other hand, point cloud networks are used for learning the anatomical structures [17,18], however, the vessel graphs in [17] are built based on Euclidean distances among the points within the vessels, which may not reflect point neighborhood along with vascular structures and could lead to wrong connections for two vessels close by. Similarly, convolutional neural network (CNN) methods such as V-Net [9] may suffer from the same problem due to Euclidean-based convolutions.

To tackle these problems, we propose a topology-aware graph network (TaG-Net) for centerline-based vessel anatomical labeling in this paper, which transforms the mask labeling problem into centerline labeling. We utilize the graph property of vessel centerlines instead of vessel masks, which is more efficient and blends the advantages of GCN and point cloud network. Prior knowledge of the vessel's tree tubular structure and anatomical information are taken into consideration. Hence, in TaG-Net, the vessel graph is constructed from the extracted centerlines, and the network's resampling and pooling layers are formed by topology-preserving sampling and topology-aware feature grouping, respectively, to preserve the graph structure during network propagation. Coupled with a point processing layer and a GCN layer, TaG-Net achieves labeling for centerlines as well as vessel masks (with back-propagation). Comparative experiments using CTA images of 401 subjects show that better labeling results can be obtained compared to state-of-the-art methods.

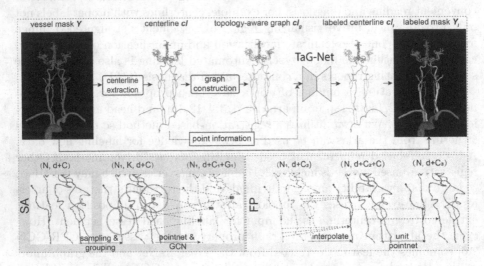

Fig. 1. Overview of our proposed TaG-Net. SA: set abstraction module; FP: feature propagation module.

2   Method

Figure 1 illustrates the pipeline for vessel labeling using the proposed TaG-Net. First, given a vessel mask Y, the centerline cl is extracted, from which the topology-aware graph cl_g is constructed. The nodes of the graph are sampled from the centerline, and the edges represent point affinity along the vessel topology. TaG-Net then takes the graph as its input, also including the coordinates and corresponding neighborhood size of each graph node/point. The output of TaG-Net is the label of each node/point of the topology-aware graph cl_g. Finally, labeled mask Y_l can be computed by back-propagating the labeled centerline cl_l onto the vessel mask Y based on directional distance maps.

2.1 Vessel Centerline Extraction

Vessel centerline can better represent the topological structure of the arteries of the head and neck, and herein we focus on labeling vessel centerline rather than processing vessel masks or original CTA images. It also reduces the complexity of the model. We start from the vessel masks obtained from the CTA images annotated by two experts for training the proposed network. In the testing stage, the vessel masks are obtained by applying a segmentation network. For both cases, a classic and efficient three-dimensional thinning algorithm [7] is performed to extract the centerlines cl from the mask Y, as shown in Fig. 1. Then, an octree data structure of 3 lattice points are constructed to refine the local connectivity of the vessel structures. The process sweeps through the octree to clean up the centerlines iteratively until desirable skeletons cl can be obtained, which preserves the topological and geometrical conditions.

2.2 Topology-Aware Graph Construction

After getting the vessel centerline cl, a topology-aware graph cl_g can be constructed by defining the nodes and edges. The topology-aware graph is the one that reflects the anatomically and topologically connected blood flows. Suppose a node can be represented by a point on the vessel centerline, it can have one edge if it is at the end of the branch, two edges in most common situations, i.e., within a blood vessel, or have three or more edges at the bifurcation or junction points. Here, the classic nearest neighbor searching method KDTree [8] is utilized to construct the tree data structure from the centerline. Each node of the KDTree represents an axis-aligned hyperrectangle. The set of points can be split by sliding the midpoint. Given any point, its r closest neighbors can be queried to construct the initial vessel graph. Post-processing of removing the redundant edges such as triangles is employed on the initial graph.

2.3 Topology-Aware Graph Network for Centerline Labeling

Once the vessel graph is constructed, a topology-aware graph network (TaG-Net) is proposed for centerline labeling by combining the idea of point cloud representation learning and GCN learning. Figure 1 shows the framework of TaG-Net. Basically, features of centerline points are extracted through the point cloud analysis block, and graph convolution is performed by offering the topological connections of nodes. The basic structure of the network is adapted from Point-Net++ [11], which consists of a hierarchical encoder and decoder architecture to achieve point cloud analysis. The encoder is composed of a number of set abstraction (SA) modules, while the decoder is formed by a series of feature propagation (FP) modules.

The SA module consists of four types of operators: sampling, grouping, pointnet, and GCN. As illustrated in Fig. 1, SA takes an $N \times (d + C)$ matrix and the graph adjacency matrix A as the input, where N is the number of points, d represents the d-dimensional point information including the coordinates and radius, which is computed from the mask, and C is the number of features. The output of the SA module is an $N_1 \times (d + C_1 + G_1)$ matrix and an new graph adjacency matrix A_1. It can be seen that SA reconstructs the input N-point graph A into an output graph A_1 with N_1 points, where the N_1 subsampled points are with d-dimensional point information and C_1-dimensional features. The four operators are described in detail as follows.

Topology-Preserving Sampling (TPS). TPS is designed for preserving the topological structures and the graph adjacency. It is the basic operation wherever the graph needs to be resampled. For this purpose, the *sampling layer* chooses a set of points from input points, which are considered the centroids of the feature grouping regions. Take an example in the *set abstraction* module, a graph with N_1 nodes can be sampled from the graph with N nodes without changing the topology of the original centerline structures. Specifically, nodes whose degree (number of edges) is not two are considered special nodes, which represent bifurcations, start points or endpoints. They make a great contribution to the topology of the vessel structure and are anatomical landmarks for vessel labeling, thus should remain after graph resampling. Since the average number of special points from the topology-aware graphs is about 350 in our dataset, the minimal number of points sampled is set to 512, which can preserve the topology of the whole vascular structure. The rest of the points are those along with the blood flow and can be sampled using iterative farthest point sampling (FPS) [11]. FPS samples the most distant points so that they spread through the centerlines and better cover the entire artery structure. To sum up, mixed TPS and FPS are utilized in the sampling layer.

Topology-Aware Grouping. As illustrated in *set abstraction* part of Fig. 1, instead of grouping points in the ball query region like [11], we propose a topology-aware grouping method to only group points with direct or indirect connection in the ball query region. The *grouping layer* takes the $N \times (d + C)$ matrix and graph adjacency matrix A as the input, and the output includes groups of points of size $N_1 \times K \times (d + C)$ where K is the number of points in the topology-aware neighborhood of the centroid points. As shown in Fig. 1, purple points along the vascular structure in the purple ball are grouped instead of all the points in the ball. This makes sure that the message only passes between the inter-label or intra-label with anatomical junction and prevents the influence of closer Euclidean-distance but farther graph-path points, which can help to handle the gaps in the computed centerlines.

The Pointnet and GCN Layer. This layer is used to process features of points. It uses a mini-PointNet [10] to encode local topological patterns within the graph. The *GCN layer* is one layer of GCN module [6]. The *pointnet layer* takes the $N_1 \times K \times (d + C)$ matrix and graph adjacency matrix A as the input, and the output has a size of $N_1 \times (d + C_1)$. The input of *GCN layer* is graph adjacency matrix A and N nodes with features from the *pointnet layer*. The output has size of $N_1 \times G_1$. Features of the *point layer* and the *GCN layer* are concatenated, whose size is $N_1 \times (d + C_1 + G_1)$, to be the input of the next SA module or the decoder.

Point Feature Propagation (FP). While SA can down-sample graphs, the FP module needs to achieve up-sampling. The FP module is built up with two layers: the *interpolating layer* and the *unit pointnet layer*. As displayed in Fig. 1, the *interpolating layer* propagates feature to the up-sampled points with size $N \times (d+C)$ by interpolating features of $N_1 \times (d+C_2)$ using inverse distance weighted average based on topological neighbors. The interpolated features of N points are then concatenated with skip-linked features from the corresponding SA module. Then, the concatenated features with $N \times (d + C_2 + C)$ are sent to the *unit pointnet layer*. The function of this layer is like 1×1 convolution in CNN. This process is repeated until the features are propagated to the original set of points. After the last FP module, the fully connected layer is utilized to label each point.

2.4 Vessel Mask Labeling

After centerline labeling, the vessel mask's label can be computed by back-propagating the centerline labels onto the vessel mask Y based on directional distance maps. Distance maps of each labeled centerline can be computed so each point on the vessel mask Y has 18 distances corresponding to 18 labels, and the label of vessel mask point can be simply assigned the label that has the smallest distance. However, the radius of different head and neck vessel segments varies, which leads to some labels of segments with smaller radii can be infected by the nearby segments with larger radii. So directional distance map is used here. The vessel mask is taken into consideration to add a large value on the distance map where the points belong to the background, and the vessel orientation is also taken into account, similar to the gradient vector flow in [15].

3   Experiments

Dataset. Experiments are conducted using our in-house head and neck CTA dataset. A total of 401 volumes of different patients are included, with in-plane image size 512×512 and slice spacing varyng from 0.361 mm to 0.707 mm. The number of slices ranges from 400 to 900, and the slice distance is 0.4–0.7 mm. Head and neck arteries were manually marked with different labels for different segments by a radiologist, and reviewed by a senior radiologist. After extracting the centerline, the label of each centerline point is determined by the same overlapping label. A five-fold cross-validation strategy is used to evaluate all subjects in the dataset.

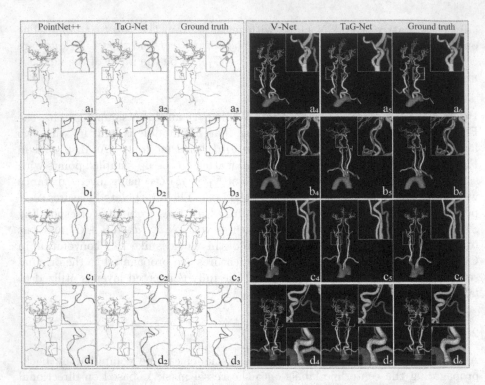

Fig. 2. Results of centerline labeling (left panel) and vessel labeling (right panel) for four samples. Each line represents one patient, the viewpoint and zoom-in regions for centerlines and vessel masks may vary.

Experiment Setup. The network architectures of TaG-Net are formed by four SA modules and four FP modules. The distance r to find the closest neighbors was set as 1.75 *voxel* in Sect. 2.2, in which the points and radius were in the original. In Sect. 2.3, the numbers of sampled points for constructing the topology-aware graph were 4096, 2048, 1024, and 512 for different SA blocks. In the training and testing, point coordinates and corresponding radii were normalized. In grouping layers, multi-resolution grouping is utilized as [11] and the radii of ball querying were set as 0.1, 0.2, 0.4, and 0.8. V-Net used to train the labeling model took the vessel mask as the input, the labeled mask as the supervision information, and Dice as the loss.

Qualitative Results. Qualitative results for centerline labeling and vessel labeling of four patients are demonstrated in Fig. 2. Each row shows the results of the same subject. The left part includes centerline labeling results of PointNet++ [11], TaG-Net, and ground truth. The right part shows vessel labeling results of V-Net [9], TaG-Net, and ground truth. The rectangles on the images stand for some comparative results. As shown in a and b, centerlines have wrong connections in a_3 and b_3 because of the adhesion in the vessel binary mask.

Table 1. The quantitative results of centerline labeling and vessel labeling. *TaG-Net w/o* represents the proposed TaG-Net without using the GCN layer.

Label	Centerline									Vessel	
	PointNet++ [11]			TaG-Net w/o			TaG-Net			V-Net [9]	TaG-Net
	Recall	Precision	F1	Recall	Precision	F1	Recall	Precision	F1	Dice	Dice
AOAR	0.934	0.981	0.957	0.971	0.976	0.973	0.986	0.973	0.979	0.995	0.998
BCT	0.937	0.976	0.956	0.921	0.934	0.927	0.917	0.915	0.916	0.959	0.982
R-CCA	0.935	0.969	0.95	0.969	0.971	0.969	0.964	0.984	0.974	0.983	0.991
L-CCA	0.927	0.954	0.940	0.964	0.968	0.965	0.976	0.977	0.977	0.98	0.988
R-ICA	0.919	0.960	0.939	0.957	0.964	0.960	0.979	0.975	0.977	0.987	0.993
L-ICA	0.912	0.969	0.939	0.968	0.971	0.969	0.973	0.984	0.978	0.971	0.987
R-VA	0.955	0.979	0.967	0.974	0.981	0.967	0.977	0.989	0.990	0.991	0.995
L-VA	0.951	0.973	0.962	0.982	0.985	0.967	0.983	0.992	0.991	0.990	0.996
BA	0.662	0.744	0.700	0.796	0.811	0.803	0.888	0.900	0.894	0.947	0.986
R-SA	0.960	0.980	0.970	0.979	0.981	0.970	0.979	0.992	0.986	0.985	0.994
L-SA	0.939	0.975	0.956	0.971	0.980	0.975	0.975	0.989	0.982	0.984	0.993
R-ECA	0.943	0.963	0.953	0.981	0.979	0.980	0.992	0.983	0.987	0.976	0.991
L-ECA	0.932	0.960	0.946	0.984	0.978	0.981	0.995	0.971	0.983	0.973	0.991
Average-neck	0.916	0.953	0.933	0.955	0.960	0.957	**0.970**	**0.971**	**0.970**	0.979	**0.991**
R-PCA	0.934	0.981	0.957	0.987	0.984	0.985	0.994	0.988	0.991	0.989	0.994
L-PCA	0.938	0.965	0.951	0.989	0.983	0.986	0.994	0.988	0.991	0.951	0.981
ACA	0.984	0.990	0.987	0.988	0.992	0.990	0.996	0.998	0.991	0.984	0.992
R-MCA	0.992	0.996	0.993	0.994	0.997	0.995	0.997	0.999	0.998	0.992	0.998
L-MCA	0.987	0.989	0.988	0.992	0.994	0.993	0.999	0.998	0.999	0.994	0.997
Average-head	0.967	0.984	0.975	0.990	0.990	0.990	**0.996**	**0.994**	**0.994**	0.982	**0.993**
Average	0.930	0.961	0.945	0.966	0.969	0.968	**0.977**	**0.977**	**0.977**	0.980	**0.991**

These wrong connections result in wrong label prediction as shown in a_1, a_4 and b_1 and b_4. However, our TaG-Net can label the adhesion region accurately as shown in a_2, a_5 and b_2, b_5. In additional, labeling results can be wrong even there is no adhesion as shown in c_1, c_4 and d_1, d_4. This may suffer from the small interval distance of the two regions. Compared with the results of TaG-Net in c_2, c_5 and d_2, d_5, It proves that TaG-Net can achieve good performance both on centerline labeling and vessel labeling. Note that, unlike previous works which use expensive vessel volume labels, we only use centerline labels to deal with the vessel volume labeling task, which is much cheaper on labeling and more computation efficient.

Quantitative Results. Table 1 reports the detailed performance of our dataset. It can be seen that TaG-Net improved average recall, precision, and F1 values for 4.7%, 1.6%, and 3.2% compared to PointNet++ [11] in centerline labeling. The results indicate that our TaG-Net performs well on centerline labeling, and the proposed strategies are effective. For vessel mask labeling, compared to V-Net which directly labels masks, the average Dice coefficient of TaG-Net increased by 1.1% and improved in all 18 segments. It is worth noting that the high Dice might be because most voxels in the masks are corrected labeled or the proportion of incorrectly labeled voxels is smaller compared to the size of the vessel mask. Moreover, we used manual masks to generate centerlines for testing the performance of centerline labeling so that the effects of segmentation errors can be eliminated. Our future work will focus on evaluating the performance of the entire segmentation and labeling pipeline as shown in Fig. 1. Regarding to efficiency, the training time is about 9 h until convergence. The test time of one case spends about 28 s. While the training time using V-Net takes about 3 days and one case testing spends about 47 s. It proves that our proposed method is more efficient than the V-Net.

4   Conclusion

This paper proposed a topology-aware graph network for centerline-based vessel labeling of 18 segments in head and neck vessels. Instead of processing the mask labeling using CNNs, we label the points of the centerline and vessel labels can be obtained by back-propagating centerline labels to vessel masks. The construction of topology-aware graph, topology-preserving sampling, topology-aware grouping, and point cloud learning combined with the GCN learning contribute important steps in the anatomical labeling of vessel centerlines. Experiments showed that compared with the centerline labeling methods using our proposed method and vessel mask labeling with V-Net, our approach achieved better accuracy. Thus, it is feasible for automatic and accurate analysis of head and neck CTA. Future work will focus on segmentation and extraction of centerlines from head and neck CTA images.

Acknowledgements. This work was supported in part by the National Key Research and Development Program of China under Grant 2018YFC0116400.

References

1. Bogunović, H., Pozo, J.M., Cárdenes, R., San Román, L., Frangi, A.F.: Anatomical labeling of the Circle of Willis using maximum a posteriori probability estimation. IEEE Trans. Med. Imaging **32**(9), 1587–1599 (2013)
2. Cao, Q., et al.: Automatic identification of coronary tree anatomy in coronary computed tomography angiography. Int. J. Cardiovasc. Imaging **33**(11), 1809–1819 (2017). https://doi.org/10.1007/s10554-017-1169-0
3. Chen, L., Hatsukami, T., Hwang, J.-N., Yuan, C.: Automated intracranial artery labeling using a graph neural network and hierarchical refinement. In: Martel, A.L., et al. (eds.) MICCAI 2020. LNCS, vol. 12266, pp. 76–85. Springer, Cham (2020). https://doi.org/10.1007/978-3-030-59725-2_8
4. Hampe, N., Wolterink, J.M., Collet, C., Planken, N., Išgum, I.: Graph attention networks for segment labeling in coronary artery trees. In: Medical Imaging 2021: Image Processing, vol. 11596, pp. 410–416. SPIE (2021)
5. Hedblom, A.: Blood vessel segmentation for neck and head computed tomography angiography (2013)
6. Kipf, T.N., Welling, M.: Semi-supervised classification with graph convolutional networks. arXiv preprint arXiv:1609.02907 (2016)

7. Lee, T.C., Kashyap, R.L., Chu, C.N.: Building skeleton models via 3-D medial surface axis thinning algorithms. CVGIP Graph. Models Image Process. **56**(6), 462–478 (1994)
8. Maneewongvatana, S., Mount, D.M.: Analysis of approximate nearest neighbor searching with clustered point sets. arXiv preprint cs/9901013 (1999)
9. Milletari, F., Navab, N., Ahmadi, S.A.: V-Net: fully convolutional neural networks for volumetric medical image segmentation. In: 2016 Fourth International Conference on 3D Vision (3DV), pp. 565–571. IEEE (2016)
10. Qi, C.R., Su, H., Mo, K., Guibas, L.J.: PointNet: deep learning on point sets for 3D classification and segmentation. In: Proceedings of the IEEE Conference on Computer Vision and Pattern Recognition, pp. 652–660 (2017)
11. Qi, C.R., Yi, L., Su, H., Guibas, L.J.: PointNet++: deep hierarchical feature learning on point sets in a metric space. Adv. Neural Inf. Process. Syst. **30** (2017)
12. Robben, D., et al.: Simultaneous segmentation and anatomical labeling of the cerebral vasculature. Med. Image Anal. **32**, 201–215 (2016)
13. Shen, M., et al.: Automatic cerebral artery system labeling using registration and key points tracking. In: Li, G., Shen, H.T., Yuan, Y., Wang, X., Liu, H., Zhao, X. (eds.) KSEM 2020. LNCS (LNAI), vol. 12274, pp. 355–367. Springer, Cham (2020). https://doi.org/10.1007/978-3-030-55130-8_31
14. Wu, D., et al.: Automated anatomical labeling of coronary arteries via bidirectional tree LSTMs. Int. J. Comput. Assist. Radiol. Surg. **14**(2), 271–280 (2019). https://doi.org/10.1007/s11548-018-1884-6
15. Xu, C., Prince, J.L.: Snakes, shapes, and gradient vector flow. IEEE Trans. Image Process. **7**(3), 359–369 (1998)
16. Yang, H., Zhen, X., Chi, Y., Zhang, L., Hua, X.S.: CPR-GCN: conditional partial-residual graph convolutional network in automated anatomical labeling of coronary arteries. In: Proceedings of the IEEE/CVF Conference on Computer Vision and Pattern Recognition, pp. 3803–3811 (2020)
17. Yao, L., et al.: Graph convolutional network based point cloud for head and neck vessel labeling. In: Liu, M., Yan, P., Lian, C., Cao, X. (eds.) MLMI 2020. LNCS, vol. 12436, pp. 474–483. Springer, Cham (2020). https://doi.org/10.1007/978-3-030-59861-7_48
18. Zhang, X., Cui, Z., Feng, J., Song, Y., Wu, D., Shen, D.: CorLab-Net: anatomical dependency-aware point-cloud learning for automatic labeling of coronary arteries. In: Lian, C., Cao, X., Rekik, I., Xu, X., Yan, P. (eds.) MLMI 2021. LNCS, vol. 12966, pp. 576–585. Springer, Cham (2021). https://doi.org/10.1007/978-3-030-87589-3_59

Transforming Connectomes to "Any" Parcellation via Graph Matching

Qinghao Liang[1]([✉]), Javid Dadashkarimi[2], Wei Dai[3], Amin Karbasi[2,4], Joseph Chang[5], Harrison H. Zhou[5], and Dustin Scheinost[1,5,6]([✉])

[1] Department of Biomedical Engineering, Yale University, New Haven, USA
{qinghao.liang,dustin.scheinost}@yale.edu
[2] Department of Computer Science, Yale University, New Haven, USA
[3] Department of Epidemiology and Public Health, Yale University, New Haven, USA
[4] Department of Electrical Engineering, Yale University, New Haven, USA
[5] Department of Statistics and Data Science, Yale University, New Haven, USA
[6] Department of Radiology and Biomedical Imaging, Yale School of Medicine, New Haven, USA

Abstract. Brain connectomes—the structural or functional connections between distinct brain regions—are widely used for neuroimaging studies. However, different ways of brain parcellation are proposed and used by different research groups without any consensus of their superiority. The variety of choices in brain parcellation makes data sharing and result comparison between studies difficult. Here, we propose a framework for transforming connectomes from one parcellation to another to address this problem. The optimal transport between nodes of two parcellations is learned in a data-driven way using graph matching methods. Spectral embedding is applied to the source connectomes to obtain node embeddings. These node embeddings are then transformed into the target space using the optimal transport. The target connectomes are estimated using the transformed node embeddings. We test the effectiveness of the proposed framework by learning the optimal transport based on data from the Human Connectome Project Young Adult, and applying it to structural connectomes data from the Lifespan Human Connectome Project Development. The efficacy of our approach is validated by comparing the estimated connectomes against their counterparts (connectomes generated directly from the target parcellation) and testing the pre-trained predictive models on estimated connectomes. We show that the estimated connectomes are highly correlated with the actual data, and predictive models for age achieve high accuracies. Overall, our proposed framework holds great promises in facilitating the generalization of connectome-based models across different parcellations.

Keywords: Graph matching · Optimal transport · Spectral embedding · Connectome

© The Author(s), under exclusive license to Springer Nature Switzerland AG 2022
L. Manfredi et al. (Eds.): ISGIE 2022/GRAIL 2022, LNCS 13754, pp. 118–127, 2022.
https://doi.org/10.1007/978-3-031-21083-9_12

1   Introduction

Recently, there has been significant interest in defining the human connectome, a comprehensive graph representation of the functional and structural connections among brain regions [2,3,12]. Yet, no consensuses exist on how to parcellate the brain into distinct regions (or the nodes in the graph) [1], resulting in connectomes of various sizes and topologies. Combining and comparing connectomes from different parcellations (and associated downstream results) is difficult given these differences in size and topology. A putative solution to this issue is to find a mapping between connectomes constructed from different parcellations. With such a mapping, a connectome based on one parcellation could be transformed to a connectome based on another parcellation, facilitating the connectomes to be combined for further analyses or comparisons between published results. In a previous study [5], a mapping between functional connectomes was proposed by learning the optimal transport between nodes using their underlying timeseries data. However, as this previous approach relied on timeseries data, rather than a connectome itself, it is not directly applicable to structural connectomes.

As connectomes can be mathematically described as weighted graphs, the connectomes transformation problem is closely related to the graph matching problem. Graph matching has been studied extensively, with applications in bioinformatics [9], computer vision [8,15], and social network analysis [16]. Indeed, the previous solution for the connectomes transformation problem [5] can be viewed as a special case of graph matching using only node information.

Inspired by [5,14], we propose Connectome to Connectome (C2C) mapping, a method to transform connectomes between two different parcellations without needing the raw data which is applicable to both functional and structural connectomes. Briefly, C2C works by, first, estimating a node representation of the connectome using a spectral embedding, then, transforming these node representations to node representations from different parcellations, and, finally, combining the transformed node representations into a symmetric functional or structural connectome. We validate C2C in two ways. First, we compare connectomes estimated from C2C against connectomes generated directly from the parcellation. We show that C2C could achieve high accuracy of estimating the target connectomes. Second, we demonstrate the utility of the reconstructed structural connectomes by using these connectomes to predict age in a developmental sample. This study extends the literature by developing a connectome mapping algorithm that is general to any type of connectome.

2   Connectome-to-Connectome (C2C) Mapping

2.1   Overview of C2C

The proposed C2C approach includes the following steps: 1) A spectral embedding of the connectomes to obtain a node representation of the connectome; 2) Node representations transformation using the optimal transport $\mathbf{T}$; and 3) Connectome reconstruction using the transformed node representations. Notably, the

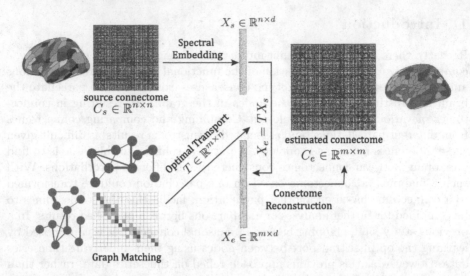

Fig. 1. Schematic of Connectome-to-Connectome (C2C) Mapping: The node representation X_s of the input connectome (parcellation α) is first obtained using spectral embedding. The optimal transport T learned on an independent dataset by graph matching is used to map X_s to the node representation X_e of the output connectome (parcellation β). The output connectome is estimated using X_e.

optimal transport can be learned on an independent dataset for increased generalizability. The whole procedure of this algorithm is shown in schematic form in the Fig. 1 and as an algorithm in Algorithm 1.

Algorithm 1: Connectome-to-Connectome (C2C)

---

1 **Input: $\mathbf{C}_s \in \mathbb{R}^{n \times n}$** - input connectome, d - the dimension of the embedding subspace, $\mathbf{T} \in \mathbb{R}^{m \times n}$ - optimal transport
2 Compute the spectral embedding $\hat{X}_s \in \mathbb{R}^{n \times d}$ of $\mathbf{C}_s$
3 Compute the transformed embedding $\hat{X}_e = \mathbf{T}\hat{X}_s$, $\hat{X}_e \in \mathbb{R}^{m \times d}$
4 Reconstruct the connectome $\hat{\mathbf{C}}_e \in \mathbb{R}^{m \times m}$ using equations in 2.5.
5 **Output: $\hat{\mathbf{C}}_e \in \mathbb{R}^{m \times m}$** - estimated connectome

---

2.2   Spectral Embedding (Algorithm 2)

C2C obtains vector representations of the nodes of a graph through spectral decomposition [7]. A weighted undirected graph is represented by a symmetric matrix $\mathbf{A} \in \mathbb{R}^{n \times n}$. Let $\hat{S}$ be the $d \times d$ diagonal matrix containing the d largest eigenvalues of $\mathbf{A}$ in magnitude on its diagonal, arranged in decreasing order (based on their actual, signed value), and let $\hat{U} \in \mathbb{R}^{n \times d}$ be a matrix containing, as columns, corresponding orthonormal eigenvectors arranged in the same order. The spectral embedding of the graph into $\mathbb{R}^d$ is defined as:

$$\mathbf{\hat{X}} = [\hat{X}_1, ..., \hat{X}_n]^T = \hat{U}|\hat{S}|^{1/2} \in \mathbb{R}^{n \times d}. \tag{1}$$

For the application to structural connectomes $\mathbf{C}_s$, $\mathbf{C}_s$ is decomposed into two parts $\mathbf{C}_s = \mathbf{C}_s^+ + \mathbf{C}_s^-$. $\mathbf{C}_s^+$ contains the positive eigenvalues of $\mathbf{C}_s$ and its spectral embedding is $\hat{U}_+ |\hat{S}_+|^{1/2} \in \mathbb{R}^{n \times d_1}$. $\mathbf{C}_s^-$ contains the negative eigenvalues of $\mathbf{C}_s$ and the spectral embedding of $-\mathbf{C}_s^-$ is $\hat{U}_- |\hat{S}_-|^{1/2} \in \mathbb{R}^{n \times d_2}$. Both $\mathbf{C}_s^+$ and $\mathbf{C}_s^-$ are used. For functional connectomes (which are positive semi-definite, correlation matrices), the spectral embedding is directly used.

Algorithm 2: Spectral Embedding

1 **Input:** $\mathbf{A} \in \mathbb{R}^{n \times n}$ - symmetrical matrix, d - the dimension of the embedding subspace
2 $U, S = eig(A)$, U is the eigenvectors and S is the eigenvalues
3 Select the largest d eigenvalues in magnitude and sorted them using original values to get $\hat{S}$. $\hat{U}$ is the corresponding eigenvectors.
4 Compute $\hat{X} = \hat{U} |\hat{S}|^{1/2} \in \mathbb{R}^{n \times d}$
5 **Output:** $\hat{X}$ - d-dimensional embedding

2.3 Gromov-Wasserstein Discrepancy

Gromov-Wasserstein Discrepancy compares graphs in a relational way, measuring how the edges in a graph compare to those in the other graph [14]. It is a natural extension of the Gromov-Wasserstein distance defined for metric-measure spaces [10]. In graph matching, a metric-measure space corresponds to the pair $(\mathbf{D}, \mathbf{u})$ of a graph $G(\mathcal{V}, \mathcal{E})$, where $\mathbf{D} = [d_{ij}] \in \mathbb{R}^{n \times n}$ represents a distance matrix derived from edge set $\mathcal{E}$, $\mathbf{u} \in \Sigma^n$ is a Borel probability measure defined on node set $\mathcal{V}$. In our case, the distance matrix is calculated using $d_{ij} = 1/(1 + c_{ij})$ from structural connectome $\mathbf{C}$ and $\mathbf{u}$ is calculated based on the normalized degree of graph. Given two graphs $G(\mathcal{V}_s, \mathcal{E}_s)$ and $G(\mathcal{V}_t, \mathcal{E}_t)$, the Gromov-Wasserstein discrepancy between $(\mathbf{D}_s, \mathbf{u}_s)$ and $(\mathbf{D}_t, \mathbf{u}_t)$ is defined as

$$d_{GW} := \min_{\mathbf{T}} \sum_{i,j,i',j'} L(d_{ij}^s, d_{i'j'}^t) T_{ii'} T_{jj'} \tag{2}$$

$L(\cdot, \cdot)$ is the square loss $L(a, b) = (a - b)^2$ and $\mathbf{T}$ is the optimal transport between the nodes of two graphs. Its elements T_{ij} represents the probability that $v_i \in \mathcal{V}_s$ matches $v_j \in \mathcal{V}_t$. The optimal transport achieves an assignment of the source nodes to the target ones. The problem could be solved through a proximal gradient method (see Algorithm 3), which decomposes a complicated non-convex optimization problem into a series of convex sub-problems.

2.4 Node-Based Mapping via Optimal Transport (Algorithm 4)

Given the corresponding node information $\mathbf{U} = [u_1^T, ..., u_d^T] \in \mathbb{R}^{n_s \times d}$ of parcellation α and $\mathbf{V} = [v_1^T, ..., v_d^T] \in \mathbb{R}^{n_t \times d}$ of parcellation as β, the optimal transport $\mathbf{T}$ is learned by solving the following equation:

$$\min_T \left\{ \sum_i C(v_i, \mathbf{T}(u_i)) : \mathbf{T}_{\sharp}\mathbf{U} = \mathbf{V} \right\} \tag{3}$$

Algorithm 3: Gromov-Wasserstein Discrepancy

1 **Input:** $\mathbf{D}_s \in \mathbb{R}^{n_s \times n_s}, \mathbf{u}_s \in \mathbb{R}^{n_s}$ - distance matrix and node distribution of source graph, $\mathbf{D}_t \in \mathbb{R}^{n_t \times n_t}, \mathbf{u}_t \in \mathbb{R}^{n_t}$ - distance matrix and node distribution of target graph

2 Compute $\mathbf{C}_{node} \in \mathbb{R}^{n_s \times n_t}, C_{ij} = |u_i^s - u_j^t|$

3 Initialize $\mathbf{T}^{(n)} = \mathbf{u}_s \mathbf{u}_t^\top$

4 **while** *not converge* **do**

5     $\mathbf{G} = e^{-(\mathbf{C}_{node} + \mathbf{L}(\mathbf{C}_s, \mathbf{C}_t, \mathbf{T}^{(n)}))/\gamma} \odot \mathbf{T}^{(n)}$

6     $\mathbf{b} = \mathbf{u}_t/(\mathbf{G}^\top \mathbf{a})$, and $\mathbf{a} = \mathbf{u}_s/(\mathbf{Gb})$

7     $\mathbf{T}^{(n+1)} = diag(\mathbf{a})\mathbf{G}diag(\mathbf{b})$

8     $n = n + 1$

9 **Output:** $\mathbf{T}^{(n)} \in \mathbb{R}^{n_s \times n_t}$

The cost matrix $C \in \mathbb{R}^{n_s \times n_t}, C_{ij} = \rho(u_i - v_j)$ measures the pairwise distance between nodes in the two parcellations, where ρ is the pearson correlation. Once estimated, $\mathbf{T}$ can be applied to u to estimate v.

Algorithm 4: Node-based Mapping via Optimal Transport

1 **Input:** $\mathbf{U} = [u_1^T, ..., u_d^T] \in \mathbb{R}^{n_s \times d}$, $\mathbf{V} = [v_1^T, ..., v_d^T] \in \mathbb{R}^{n_t \times d}$

2 Compute the cost matrix $C \in \mathbb{R}^{n_s \times n_t}, C_{ij} = \rho(u_i - v_j)$

3 **for** $i \leftarrow 1$ **to** d **do**

4   Compute $\mathbf{T}_i$ by solving Eq. (3) using Sinkhorn algorithm [5]

5 $\mathbf{T} = \sum_{i=1}^d \mathbf{T}_i/d$

6 **Output:** $\mathbf{T} \in \mathbb{R}^{n_s \times n_t}$

2.5 Connetomes Estimation

The connetomes are reconstructed from the transformed node representation. Structural connectomes are estimated using: $\hat{\mathbf{C}}_e = \hat{\mathbf{C}}_e^+ + \hat{\mathbf{C}}_e^- = \hat{\mathbf{X}}_+ \hat{\mathbf{X}}_+^T - \hat{\mathbf{X}}_- \hat{\mathbf{X}}_-^T$ and functional connectomes are estimated using: $\hat{\mathbf{C}}_e = \hat{\mathbf{X}} \hat{\mathbf{X}}^T$.

3 Results

3.1 Datasets

The optimal transports used in the experiment were learned using the functional and structural data from the Human Connectome Project (HCP) [13]. The C2C framework was validated using the optimal transports on the Lifespan Human Connectome Project Development (HCP-D). Structural connectomes were created from the Shen (268 nodes) [11], Craddock (200 nodes) [4] and Brainnetome (246 nodes) [6] parcellations.

HCP Dataset: 1) fMRI Data: We used the resting-state data from the HCP to create functional connectomes. Data with a maximum frame-to-frame displacement of 0.15 mm or greater were excluded, resulting in a sample of 876 resting-state scans. Analyses were restricted only to the LR phase encoding, which consisted of 1200 individual time points. Additional preprocessing included regressing 24 motion parameters, regressing the mean white matter, CSF, and grey matter timeseries, removing the linear trend, and low-pass filtering. For each scan, the average time series within each region was obtained. 2) **DTI Data:** We used the diffusion tensor data of 1065 subjects to create structural connectomes. After correcting for susceptibility artifacts, we applied DSI-studio to reconstruct the diffusion data using generalized q-sampling imaging and create structural connectomes with automatic fiber tracking for the six parcellations listed above.

HCP-D Dataset: The same procedure as described above was applied to the DTI data of 636 subjects to calculate structural connectomes.

3.2   Graph Matching Methods

We used three graph matching approaches to estimate the optimal transport: 1) **Gromov-Wasserstein Discrepancy(GWD)**: The optimal transport was estimated by calculating the Gromov-Wasserstein Discrepancy between each pair of structural connectomes in HCP dataset. The optimal transports were averaged across all 1065 DTI subjects to get a more robust estimation. 2) **Node-based Mapping using fMRI timeseries data (NBM_time)**: The fMRI timeseries data of each node were used as node information in Algorithm 4 as in [5]. The optimal transports were averaged across all 876 fMRI subjects. 3) **Node-based Mapping using the spectral embedding of structural connectomes (NBM_emb)**: The spectral embedding of the connectomes were used as node information in Algorithm 4. The optimal transports were averaged across all 1065 DTI subjects.

3.3   Evaluating C2C on HCP-D Structural Connectomes

We evaluated the estimation accuracy of our C2C framework on structural connectomes in HCP-D dataset. The Pearson's correlation between the estimated connectomes and the "ground-truth" structural connectomes was calculated as the metric of estimation accuracy. All three approaches achieved significant correlations between different parcellation pairs (Fig. 2; $p < 0.05$). However, the accuracy of **NBM_emb** was significantly lower than **NBM_time** and **GWD** in all cases, suggesting that the optimal transport learned on node embeddings of structural connectomes may not be reliable.

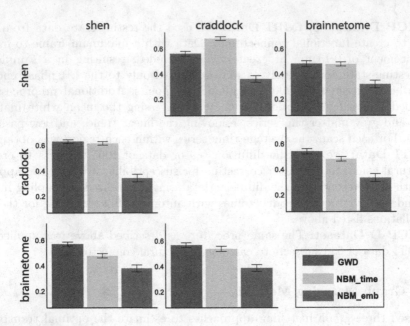

Fig. 2. The correlation between the target structural connectomes and estimated connectomes using optimal transports learned using three different graph matching approaches. Error bars are standard deviation of the correlation across all 636 subjects.

3.4   Age Prediction Using Estimated Connectomes

To further evaluated the quality of estimated structural connectomes, we showed that the predictive models of age built on original target connectomes could be generalized to connectomes estimated by C2C. In each train/test split, a ridge regression model was trained using the target connectomes to predict the age of each subject. This model was then tested on connectomes estimated using C2C. The whole process was repeated 100 times. Pearson's correlation between the true age and predicted age was used as the measurement of predictive performance. Results showed significant ($p < 0.001$) prediction accuracy using estimated connectomes (Fig. 3). Connectomes estimated using **GWD** and **NBM_time** retained 75% of the model performance on the original connectomes (the dash line), suggesting useful brain information of the connectomes were successfully preserved.

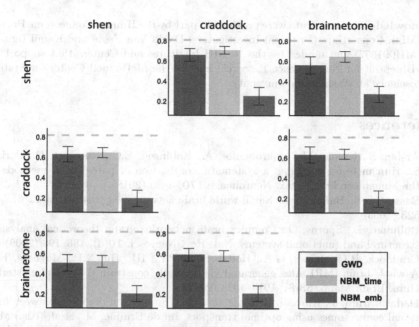

Fig. 3. Prediction results of age based on structural connectomes estimated from our proposed C2C framework. The bar plots show the Pearson's correlation r between the predicted age and true age in testing set as the measure of predictive performance. The dash line is the predictive performance using original target connectomes. Error bars are generated through 100 iterations.

1   Discussion and Conclusions

We propose a framework to transform connectomes between different parcelations without needing the raw imaging data. Using graph matching methods, an optimal transport between nodes is estimated and can be used to map node information across parcelations. The utility of our method is validated on structural connectomes in terms of estimation accuracy and downstream predictive modelling performance.

It is worth noticing that although learned through a data-driven approach, the optimal transport captures the topology structure of a parcelation and it is generalizable across datasets and imaging modalities. The optimal transports estimated by Gromov-Wasserstein discrepancy using structural connectomes and node-based mapping using fMRI timeseries data achieve consistent performance on the dataset testing.

Future work includes incorporating parcelations information into graph matching and evaluating other node embedding methods. Overall, our framework provides a novel tool for transforming connectomes of different imaging modalities.

Acknowledgements. Data were provided in part by the Human Connectome Project, WU-Minn Consortium (Principal Investigators: David Van Essen and Kamil Ugurbil; U54 MH091657) and funded by the 16 NIH Institutes and Centers that support the NIH Blueprint for Neuroscience Research; and by the McDonnell Center for Systems Neuroscience at Washington University.

References

1. Arslan, S., Ktena, S.I., Makropoulos, A., Robinson, E.C., Rueckert, D., Parisot, S.: Human brain mapping: a systematic comparison of parcellation methods for the human cerebral cortex. Neuroimage **170**, 5–30 (2018)
2. Bassett, D.S., Bullmore, E.: Small-world brain networks. Neuroscientist **12**(6), 512–523 (2006)
3. Bullmore, E., Sporns, O.: Complex brain networks: graph theoretical analysis of structural and functional systems. Nat. Rev. Neurosci. **10**(3), 186–198 (2009)
4. Craddock, R.C., James, G.A., Holtzheimer, P.E., III., Hu, X.P., Mayberg, H.S.: A whole brain fMRI atlas generated via spatially constrained spectral clustering. Hum. Brain Mapp. **33**(8), 1914–1928 (2012)
5. Dadashkarimi, J., Karbasi, A., Scheinost, D.: Data-driven mapping between functional connectomes using optimal transport. In: de Bruijne, M., et al. (eds.) MICCAI 2021. LNCS, vol. 12903, pp. 293–302. Springer, Cham (2021). https://doi.org/10.1007/978-3-030-87199-4_28
6. Fan, L., et al.: The human brainnetome atlas: a new brain atlas based on connectional architecture. Cereb. Cortex **26**(8), 3508–3526 (2016)
7. Gallagher, I., Jones, A., Bertiger, A., Priebe, C., Rubin-Delanchy, P.: Spectral embedding of weighted graphs. arXiv preprint arXiv:1910.05534 (2021)
8. Jun, S.H., Wong, S.W., Zidek, J., Bouchard-Cote, A.: Sequential graph matching with sequential Monte Carlo. In: Singh, A., Zhu, J. (eds.) Proceedings of the 20th International Conference on Artificial Intelligence and Statistics. Proceedings of Machine Learning Research, vol. 54, pp. 1075–1084. PMLR (2017)
9. Kuchaiev, O., Pržulj, N.: Integrative network alignment reveals large regions of global network similarity in yeast and human. Bioinformatics **27**(10), 1390–1396 (2011)
10. Memoli, F.: Gromov-Hausdorff distances in Euclidean spaces. In: 2008 IEEE Computer Society Conference on Computer Vision and Pattern Recognition Workshops, pp. 1–8 (2008). https://doi.org/10.1109/CVPRW.2008.4563074
11. Shen, X., Tokoglu, F., Papademetris, X., Constable, R.T.: Groupwise whole-brain parcellation from resting-state fMRI data for network node identification. Neuroimage **82**, 403–415 (2013)
12. Sporns, O., Chialvo, D.R., Kaiser, M., Hilgetag, C.C.: Organization, development and function of complex brain networks. Trends Cogn. Sci. **8**(9), 418–425 (2004)
13. Van Essen, D.C., et al.: The WU-Minn human connectome project: an overview. Neuroimage **80**, 62–79 (2013)
14. Xu, H., Luo, D., Carin, L.: Scalable Gromov-Wasserstein learning for graph partitioning and matching. In: Wallach, H., Larochelle, H., Beygelzimer, A., d' Alché-Buc, F., Fox, E., Garnett, R. (eds.) Advances in Neural Information Processing Systems, vol. 32. Curran Associates, Inc. (2019)

15. Yu, T., Yan, J., Wang, Y., Liu, W., Li, B.: Generalizing graph matching beyond quadratic assignment model. In: Bengio, S., Wallach, H., Larochelle, H., Grauman, K., Cesa-Bianchi, N., Garnett, R. (eds.) Advances in Neural Information Processing Systems, vol. 31. Curran Associates, Inc. (2018)
16. Zhang, J., Yu, P.S.: Multiple anonymized social networks alignment. In: 2015 IEEE International Conference on Data Mining, pp. 599–608 (2015)

Author Index

Printed in the United States
by Baker & Taylor Publisher Services

Printed in the United States
by Baker & Taylor Publisher Services